ESSAYS ON DETERMINISM
KENT STUDIES IN ENGLISH, NO. 1.
Under the editorship of
Howard P. Vincent

ESSAYS ON
DETERMINISM
IN AMERICAN LITERATURE

LUTHER STEARNS MANSFIELD • THOMAS E. CONNOLLY
EDWARD STONE • GAY WILSON ALLEN
EDGAR M. BRANCH • JOHN LYDENBERG
SHERWOOD CUMMINGS

Edited by

SYDNEY J. KRAUSE

THE KENT STATE UNIVERSITY PRESS

A Prefatory Note

THE PAPERS constituting this volume, the first in the series Kent Studies in English, are, with one exception, revisions of papers originally presented at the Modern Language Association Meeting in Chicago in December, 1963. Those by Edgar M. Branch, Thomas E. Connolly, Sherwood Cummings, John Lydenberg, and Edward Stone were read before the American Literature Group; the one by Gay Wilson Allen was read before the American Studies Association Group. The idea of bringing the papers together in this form originated with Martin Nurmi. Henry Nash Smith, program chairman of the American Literature Group, whom I consulted about assembling for collective publication the papers selected by him and his committee, gave encouragement which I very much appreciate.

I wish to thank each of the contributors, and particularly Luther Mansfield, who on rather short notice agreed to write an essay specifically for this volume to fill an important gap in our study of determinism. For a variety of useful suggestions I am also indebted to Howard P. Vincent, David Krause, Doris Franklin, Martin Nurmi, Julia Waida, and my wife, Evy.

Holt, Rinehart, Winston, Inc., has granted permission to reprint the passages Mr. Stone uses from Frost's "Stars" and "The Onset" (from *Complete Poems of Robert Frost*. Copyright 1923, 1934 by Holt, Rinehart and Winston, Inc. Copyright renewed 1951, © 1962 by Robert Frost).

S. J. K.

Kent State University
Kent, Ohio
July, 1964

Table of Contents

When I see the blindness and the wretchedness of man, when I regard the whole silent universe, and man without light, left to himself, and, as it were, lost in this corner of the universe, without knowing who has put him there, what he has come to do, what will become of him at death, and incapable of all knowledge, I become terrified, like a man who should be carried in his sleep to a dreadful desert island, and should awake without knowing where he is, and without means of escape. And thereupon I wonder how people in a condition so wretched do not fall into despair.

—BLAISE PASCAL, *Pensées, 692*

◆SYDNEY J. KRAUSE

Introduction

WHEN WE think of determinism, we think of a body of literature that is theoretically all of a piece, circumscribed by a rigid, even predictable, selectivity in subject, characterization, tone, ending, etc. Despite quibbles over whether it is ultimately pessimistic or optimistic,[1] or neither, there are few more easily defined of the notably amorphous "movements" in literary history than that which flows from Zola and Maupassant in France through Hardy and Butler in England to Dreiser and Farrell in America, and which customarily goes by the name Naturalism.

Specifically, deterministic naturalism brings to mind characters who move about in a moral limbo, are doomed by external forces, and seem frustratingly incapable of elevating themselves (like Dreiser's George Hurstwood or Dos Passos's Charlie Anderson).[2] One of the clichés we therefore apply to them is that they degenerate (Zola's term), rather than develop. Their world, as depicted in such works as *La Terre, Maggie, McTeague,* or *The Young Manhood of Studs Lonigan,* is oppressively sub-human. At times it is a veritable wilderness of predators and their prey, as glimpsed, for example, in the relationship in *Vandover and the Brute* between the aggressive Charlie Geary and dissolute Vandover.[3] Assuredly "God is dead," but, unlike the state envisioned by Nietzsche and Sartre, so is the spirit of man. Norris, spouting apocalyptic pronouncements toward the end of *The Octopus,* summed up the inconsequence of individual men:

1

Men were nothings, mere animalcules, mere ephemerides that fluttered and fell and were forgotten between dawn and dusk. . . . Men were naught, death was naught, life was naught; FORCE only existed—FORCE that brought men into the world, FORCE that crowded them out of it to make way for the succeeding generation.[4]

Those who got on in this Spencerian world did so by exerting their own force, in the manner of supermen and beasts. That was the elementary lesson young Cowperwood learned in the streets of Philadelphia and on viewing the unequal contest between lobster and squid; so that the exertion of force came as second nature to him in the world of finance. Henry Fleming learned a similar lesson on distinguishing himself from the "blue demonstration," and realizing that just as heroism could be built on cowardice, so ironically, did a man really "become another thing in battle."

Ideal subjects for the determinist are the banality and materiality underscored by Zola in his notes on *L'Assommoir*. Not only did he have to give Gervaise Macquart "modest desires that [would] never be realized," but he felt impelled to concentrate on "the bestial, drab, filthy side of life"; so that his might be "a story of magisterial nudity, day to day reality, going in a straight line, . . . [with] absolutely nothing romantic or affected."[5] We also recognize determinism by a certain mood; it is somber, gloomy, loveless, despairing and fatalistic (the impalpable affliction of Hardy's Wessex folk), and pervaded by images of sordidness and animalism (like those of low-lived New York in *Maggie*). Ugly and, hopefully, sensational details are pursued for their own sake, and also because Zola—borrowing from Claude Bernard—had laid a "scientific" basis for recording them in an attempt to show that the data of human existence were to be "observed" and "experimented" upon in much the same way that scientists treated purely physical phenomena. Like Clyde Griffiths or Gervaise, the heroes and heroines of deterministic literature are destined to have a bad and often ironical end, whether merited or not. Like Nana or Carrie they can be callously destructive persons, with a kind of insensitivity that it is hard to call evil. In part, the fatal endings derive from the philosophy of determinism, which self-evidently implies absolute causality, and which, from the point of view of our humanity, is pessimistic. As William James once put it, "Determinism . . . virtually defines the universe as a place in which what ought to be is impossible,—in other words, as an organism whose constitution is afflicted with an incurable taint, an irremediable flaw."[6]

While determinism is not uniquely associated with naturalism, naturalism is the only literary movement to have been dominated by it. In its times—roughly the half century between *L'Assommoir* (1877) and *An American Tragedy* (1925)—marked as they were by the ardors of Social Darwinism and the cultural alienation of the artist, naturalism was a provocative new force. It was socially pertinent, a vital challenge to Victorian stuffiness, and, above all, it had the power to communicate what Henry James called "a direct impression of life." However, compelling as it once was in these and other respects, naturalism has undergone a drastic reversal in recent years. As early as 1942, Philip Rahv was writing "Notes on the Decline of Naturalism." He suggested that its state was one of "utter debility," which had resulted, he felt, from the interest of new writers in creating an "imaginative prose" and from the "inwardness" stimulated by the psychological sciences.[7] One can point out various other reasons for the decline of naturalism—*e.g.,* since it has won most of its technical battles, as well as its battles for social reform, and has lost most of its ideological battles, none of these matters is any longer a discussible problem. But the special issue on which naturalism seems most grievously "dated," and on which it stands most in need of redemption, if it is to be worth redeeming at all, is that of determinism. For, outside the usual academic discussions of Greek tragedy, determinism, as such, simply has no status in modern criticism. Nor has it been much of a factor in modern literature and philosophy since Max Planck and Werner Heisenberg brought to light the indeterminacy of intra-atomic physics and unsettled the conventional notions of deterministic causality.

To be sure, aspects of naturalism can be found in the works of Hemingway and Faulkner. And, of course, naturalistic techniques persist in the later works of James T. Farrell, John Steinbeck, and Erskine Caldwell, as well as in the writing of Nelson Algren, Norman Mailer, James Jones, and Willard Motley, but minus the earlier reductionism and insuperable determinism. In fact, determinism is the one element that contemporary naturalists vehemently disavow. Mr. Farrell, speaking before the joint luncheon of the American Literature Group and American Studies Association at the 1963 Modern Language Association Meeting, declared more than once that he was no determinist, that he did not know what it meant to write deterministic fiction, and that the only grounds on which one might presume to use the term were those on which no author could deny he was deterministic—*i.e.,* playing God, he had predetermined what would happen in his story.

In the light of the subsequent, freer course of naturalism, the remarkable thing is that the more one examines the early, deterministic naturalism and the uses to which determinism has been put in non-naturalistic fiction, the more one perceives (a) that no such creature as a pure and thorough-going determinism has ever existed in literature—Zola notwithstanding, (b) that determinism derives most of its literary effectiveness from the presence, or at least latency, of its opposite, and (c) that the sense of human grandeur attained in traditionalist literature is often proportional to the determinism it opposes. Supporting these conclusions is the fact that historically the fears of supernaturalists like Donne and Pascal over the encroachment of the natural upon the human have had more in common with the despondency of literary naturalists than have the views of naturalistic scientists like Bacon, Newton, or Darwin.

What is attempted in this collection of essays is to broaden the reference of determinism from within and without the framework of naturalism, by noticing how much the assumptions of moral meaning in traditionalist literature are dependent on determinism, and how much the assumptions of determinism in naturalistic literature are dependent on moral meaning. As the more doctrinaire form of naturalism is the background against which determinism is discussed in these essays, it will bear closer scrutiny here.

II

There is much that escapes the deterministic blight in the works of the early naturalists, and that which does escape — as, sympathy for the defeat of human aspirations—is somewhat more important than the determinism which it offsets. Obviously, just as determinism has no meaning in the absence of a conflicting belief in free will, so can the naturalistic dehumanization of man have little meaning in the absence of compassion and a comparable feeling for what is moral and just. Thus the *effect* of naturalism is almost uniformly achieved by contrasts between indifferent forces, the laws of heredity and environment, and the human reaction to them. Moreover, setting aside theoretic and formal crudities and what now seems a naïveté of critical doctrine, we are likely to find that deterministic naturalism is in practice scarcely as formulaic, or as shabbily anti-humanistic as the propositions we can make about it—though true—would seem to suggest. As soon as we begin dipping into individual works to discover anew what naturalism has to tell us about itself, we are apprised not only of how much it varies from writer to writer and novel to novel, but especially of how the best of naturalistic fiction deviates from mechanistic principles in the preservation of moral qualities.

A brief survey of some of the more familiar naturalistic novels will provide a reference for one of the major assumptions of this collection of essays—which is that although determinism may lower the significance of Man in the abstract, it is only because determinism educes the moral and emotional mettle of particular men that it has significance for literature. Anticipating Hemingway's notion of grace under pressure, Dreiser, for example, has Lester Kane maintain that as pawns of circumstance "the best we can do is to hold our personality intact."

Clearly, the Dreiser of *Sister Carrie* and *Jennie Gerhardt* is different from the Dreiser who gives us the rise and fall of Nietzschean *Übermensch* in the Trilogy of Desire. Yet in either the passively sacrificial or the vigorously assertive mood, his chief characters, if tarnished, still come through as human beings who somehow transcend the events determining their fate. For all the talk about Cowperwood's indifference to right and wrong and for all his unscrupulous financial deals and philandering, Dreiser cannot help making him an attractive hero. He succeeds because he is strong, ambitious, intelligent, and self-reliant. He can be "humane and democratic," "tender and sympathetic" to his mother, and before the Chicago fire and the panic he had had "the freshness of spring evenings in him." Dreiser himself becomes infatuated with him, remarking as Cowperwood sits in his jail cell: "It is only when the soul of man has been built up into some strange self-confidence, some curious faith in its own powers, based, no doubt, on the actual presence of these same powers subtly involved in the body, that it fronts life unflinchingly."[8] With the girls, there is sadness of heart over the way their pliant natures are taken advantage of. Carrie Meeber—not quite meek and not quite eager—when faced by impending starvation and further humiliation in staying with Hurstwood, does more than rescue herself in becoming an actress; in rising, she creates her own identity. Unlike Carrie, poor Jennie is the very soul of virtue and devotion. The trouble is, as Dreiser says, "the world into which Jennie was . . . unduly thrust forth was that in which virtue has always vainly struggled since time immemorial."[9] Although fate deals rather cruelly with her by putting her in the way of two wealthy and influential men, who become interested in her, seduce her, and cannot marry her, she remains faithful to the second of them, Lester Kane, and is rewarded by attending him during his last days and learning that it was she alone he loved. Dreiser does not denigrate the human spirit. Rather, he complains that as "we live in an age in which the impact of materialized forces is well-nigh irresistible; the spiritual nature is overwhelmed by the shock."[10]

Much the same concern for the human spirit and departure from a relentless determinism can be found in representative works of his predecessors, Garland, Norris, and Crane. While Garland maintained a bleak outlook in *Main-Travelled Roads* and *A Son of the Middle Border, Rose of Dutcher's Coolly,* proceeding from the same background, is a virtual success story. The motherless heroine, who must fend for herself rather early, refuses to be overcome by either her environment or her own emotions, and with an exceptional display of pertinacity gets her education, finds herself as a writer and makes men accept her on her own terms. As Garland said, Rose Dutcher was not to be a "victim" because she was "quite evidently a proud, strong woman."[11] When Norris entered the phase of his romantic naturalism in *The Octopus* and *The Pit,* he injected a new value into the struggle for life by deifying the fecundity of Nature. It produced "life out of death eternity . . . out [of] dissolution."[12] Consequently, the farmers who were slain did *not* die for "naught." Being growers of the wheat, they had a moral cause, which in Norris's philosophic interludes almost overshadows their economic grievances against the Railroad. As Vanamee assures Presley, just before the wheat swallows up the villainous Behrman, agent of the Railroad (as it will later ruin the speculator, Curtis Jadwin), "the good never dies; evil dies, cruelty, oppression, selfishness, greed—these die; but nobility, but love, but sacrifice, but generosity, but truth . . . these live forever, these are eternal."[13] Unremittingly pessimistic as Crane could be in suggesting the ironies that fate plays on innocent persons, and in exposing the low moral character of ordinary people in Whilomville, he probably went further than other naturalists in celebrating the moral courage of individuals, as he did with Henry Johnson and his benefactor, Dr. Trescott, in *The Monster;* with the initiation of Henry Fleming; and with the "subtle brotherhood" of the men in "The Open Boat." It must also be said of the pathetic Maggie, who "blossomed in a mud puddle," that if her mother did not think her a "pearl dropped unstained into Rum Alley from Heaven," the reader recognizes her as the only good person there and regards her suicide as a moral victory over the slums, her mother, her boy friend, and her life on the streets.

British naturalism tends to be either more pathetic (in the manner of George Moore), more fatalistic (in the manner of Thomas Hardy), or simply more contemplative and detached (in the manner of Samuel Butler) than the American and French varieties. In no other phase of naturalism is man's moral being more nobly vindicated. Backed by a long tradition of humanism and the example of Tennyson and Browning in making evolution subtend spiritual progress, the British naturalists all but neutralized determinism by stressing the willfulness and dogged strength of character it brought out in its victims. Esther Waters is the Richardsonian heroine manqué. The only differences are that she falls and is subjected to a greater variety of hazards. But endowed with strong reserves of native virtue, she cares for her illegitimate son regardless of her own destitution and is rewarded in the end by seeing him become a handsome soldier. A happy, morally satisfying ending also awaits Ernest Pontifex in *The Way of All Flesh,* after his idealistic rebellions against parents and Church, his loss of money, imprisonment, and misguided romance. Lamarckism is treated quite speculatively by the narrator, who holds that Ernest's indiscretions were not due to heredity, but to his own poor judgment; and Butler's naturalism—tempered by vitalism—threatened his hero without demolishing him. Hardy, of course, seems a formidable determinist, but for the most part, he looks upon determinism more in sadness than in anger. In perspective, it is no exaggeration to say that, morally, the uncomplaining stoicism with which Tess Durbeyfield, Michael Henshard, and Jude Frawley bear up under outrageously circumstantial misfortune makes a shambles of the blind fatality that does them in. Henshard is in fact regenerated ("How will you forgive all my roughness in former days?" he asks Elizabeth-Jane before the catastrophe of Newson's return).[14] His moral dignity rising as his fortunes decline, he dies a tragic hero.

Confronting Zola, the bête noire himself, one must be prepared to accept both Oscar Cargill's judgment that he made "degeneracy . . . the common history of man" and Lars Ähnebrink's judgment that "at heart, he was an optimistic Utopian, whose temperament clashed with the naturalistic formula."[15] If Zola degraded man, he did so in hopes of alarming and thereby improving him. He was as fully committed to meliorism as were any of the well known expositors of positivism and evolution ranging from Comte and Lyell to Spencer, Huxley, and Fiske. Zola believed that the knowledge gained from an experimental novelist's studies in human behavior would eventually lead to moral wisdom and the ability of scientists to control man and society for their mutual goods.[16] Furthermore, borrowing Bernard's distinction between determinism and fatalism, Zola rejected fatalism because it did not, as determinism did, provide for change. His works offer the best testimony to his humanitarian moralism. In *L'Assommoir*—which he called "simply a lesson in morality"—Zola warned against the evils of drink, and the hereditary scars it left; in *Nana* against the moral and physical ruination attendant upon lust; in *Germinal* against the viciousness of exploitive capitalism; in *La Terre* against the degenerative effects of remorseless greed; and in *Le Débacle* against the bestiality of war and the demoralization of the Army under vacillating leadership. In each instance, Zola's social criticism would have been empty and his theme lost were it not for the sympathy, and in some cases, admiration that he generated for such basically decent persons as Gervaise, Madame Hugon, Rose Mignon, Etienne Lantier, Jean Macquart, Francoise Mouche, Maurice Levasseur, his sister Henrietta, and her poor brave husband, Weiss. Even amidst the sickening brutishness of *La Terre,* which caused five of his disciples to publicly repudiate him, Zola excites such strong moral feelings on behalf of old Fouan, who parcelled out his land among his three children only to be cruelly maltreated by them, that his Lear-like suffering practically becomes a redemptive experience. In addition, Zola lightens the animalism and humanizes the grossness of his peasants by surrounding them with outrageously Rabelaisian situations. (Hyacinth, for example, Fouan's oldest son, who is irreverently called "Jesus Christ," is noted for his uproarious scatalogical exploits.) Nor are Zola's heroes necessarily deprived of human dignity. After the starvation, physical punishment, betrayals and final defeat inflicted upon the miners in *Germinal* and the soldiers in *Le Débacle*, Zola concludes on a hopeful, one might even say a triumphant, note. Etienne goes off to Paris resolved that having profited from his experience, he will be a leader of working men; and Jean Macquart, having found love, must nonetheless bid farewell to Henrietta and do what he can to help rebuild the nation. Far from being broken, the spirit of these men is immeasurably enhanced by all they have endured.

In sum, the characteristic mood of deterministic naturalism is mixed and paradoxical. Its key paradox centers on the brute refusal of the human to be sucked down into the vortex of natural law. It is because of their cheerless prospects that we are cheered by the moral drive of individual characters who suffer much, but who like Jean Macquart, Esther Waters, or Rose Dutcher still manage to hold themselves intact as human beings despite the animal ruthlessness of others and the natural and social causalities that confine them. In one of his strategic asides, Dreiser contemplated one cause of this paradox in reasoning that is interestingly reminiscent of the Great Chain of Being.

Our civilization is still in a middle stage, scarcely beast, in that it is no longer wholly guided by instinct; scarcely human, in that it is not yet wholly guided by reason. On the tiger no responsibility rests. We see him aligned by nature with the forces of life—he is born into their keeping and without thought he is protected. We see man far removed from the lairs of the jungles, his innate instincts dulled by too near an approach to free-will, his free will not sufficiently developed to replace his instincts and afford him perfect guidance. He is becoming too wise to hearken always to instincts and desires; he is still too weak to always prevail against them. As a beast, the forces of life aligned him with them; as a man, he has not yet wholly learned to align himself with the forces. In this intermediate stage he wavers—neither drawn in harmony with nature by his instincts nor yet wisely putting himself into harmony by his own free will. He is even as a wisp in the wind, moved by every breath of passion, acting now by his will and now by his instincts, erring with one, only to retrieve by the other, falling by one, only to rise by the other—a creature of incalculable variability.[17]

III

The variability of literary determinism has not gone unrecognized.[18] For one thing, because of naturalism's inner defiance of its own stereotypes, almost everyone who has tried to reconcile naturalistic theory with naturalistic practice has been impressed by how little the one accounts for the other. Charles C. Walcutt, for example, speaks of the "divided stream" of naturalism, the manifestations of which he describes as protean; and when he deals with individual writers he is compelled to classify their works into as many as four subtypes. Philip Rahv has also seen the course of naturalism as moving in at least two directions, one towards "passive documentation" and the other towards the "exposure of socioeconomic conditions"; while Lars Ähnebrink, summing up the "varied nature" and "heterogeneous character" of American naturalism in the nineties, spoke of its being "full of inconsistencies, [with] strong ethical characters . . . contrasted with weak, passive figures dominated by forces beyond their control, . . . realism [mingled] with lyricism, *Tendenz* with objectivity." Among other like appraisals of naturalism, one finds Willard Thorp noting the vast differences between such naturalists as Norris and Mailer and attributing the persistence of naturalism in the twentieth century to "its essential flexibility"; Edward Wagenknecht remarking the contradictions and "romantic" elements in naturalism; Malcolm Cowley declaring that most naturalists are really "dreamers," "tender minded" persons who "write shocking books because they have been [morally] shocked"; and Donald Pizer ascribing the "continuing strength" of naturalism in America to its lack of a coherent "philosophic center."[19]

One matter which helps to account for the looseness amidst apparent rigidity in the naturalists' handling of determinism is that they paid only lip-service to Darwinian meliorism, if they recognized it at all. Darwin and Huxley had credited man's rational, sympathetic, and moral faculties with placing him at the top of the evolutionary scale, in the most favored position in the natural world.[20] The naturalists were dubious, however, that man could exercise his higher nature in a world where blind forces seemed to nurture his lower nature. If they dwelt on the process by which man was returned to the condition of nature, they also showed that he resisted it, and that resistance brought out the best in him.

Note, for example, how Norris glorifies Curtis Jadwin, the "Great Bull," at the climactic moment when he is about to be broken, as irrepressible Nature inundates him with wheat and ruins his efforts to make a corner in it.

Blind and insensate, Jadwin strove against the torrent of the Wheat. There in the middle of the Pit, surrounded and assaulted by herd after herd of wolves yelping for his destruction, he stood braced, rigid upon his feet, his head up, his hand, the great bony hand that once had held the whole Pit in its grip, flung high in the air, in a gesture of defiance, while his voice like the clangour of bugles sounding to the charge of the forlorn hope, rang out again and again, over the din of his enemies.[21]

So long as their characters struggle to obtain personal equilibrium, or arouse pity when they have lost it, the naturalists create the tensions that distinguish all types of literature in which determinism has figured artistically. After all, man cannot be juxtaposed with universal powers without gaining more than he loses.

Aspects of these tensions between what is naturally determined and what is nevertheless willed and felt by men form the starting point and common denominator for these *Essays on Determinism*. Each critic dispenses with what Edgar Branch calls the "bulldozer view of determinism" and in one way or another attempts to quicken the original presentiment of conflict with which, from the time of Sophocles, writers have traditionally approached determinism. No attempt is made at comprehensiveness; rather, the intention is to offer representative contemporary attitudes towards determinism, with the hope that a post-naturalistic perspective may help to remind us of its function as a source of dramatic action.

The essays are presented in three groups. In the first, Luther Stearns Mansfield and Thomas E. Connolly show how determinism operates in the respectively pre- and post-naturalistic fiction of Melville and Faulkner. Mansfield considers the most ambitious treatment of the interaction between free will and determinism in all of nineteenth-century American fiction. Using the "Mat-Maker" chapter in Moby-Dick as a metaphor of the "essential materials" Melville worked with as fabulist, Mansfield notes the various patterns he wove from "the warp of necessity and the woof of free will." Like Emerson, Melville had insisted on the "supremacy of self," particularly when deterministic contingencies compelled men to make the difficult choices that Tommo, Taji, Ahab, Pierre, and Captain Vere had to make. The acutest frustrations suffered by the noble self occurred when it felt itself hemmed in and its fate determined by the "joint stock company" called human society, by its cultural heritage, or, worse still, by its immediate psychic heredity. Excruciating conundrums might be posed by irrational Chance, but Mansfield shows that, regardless of obstacles, Melville's heroes persevere in their search for "personal identity in the snarled yarns of the Loom of Time," and that the best of them accept the consequences of their fatal choices. Thomas Connolly examines certain of Faulkner's heroes in the light of a hereditary, environmental and psychologically imposed fate, which at once fixes their character and the outcome of their lives. It was a sort of "naturalistic" determinism (much like Norris's) which led Faulkner to reflect that "the individual is not too much, he's only a pinch of dust, he won't be here very long anyway, but his species, his dreams, they go on." At any rate, the sense of fatality, which Connolly holds is strongest in the early works, invests the stories of such haunted figures as Bayard Sartoris, Quentin Compson, and Joe Christmas with a tragic significance that fate alone—determined by their social code and collective past—can give them.

In the second group, Edward Stone and Gay Wilson Allen consider some symbolic and philosophic ramifications of determinism. Stone investigates a shift in the symbolism of whiteness, which, with the assistance of nineteenth-century determinism, begins to lose some of its connotations of beauty, purity, and virtue and to take on those of blankness, emptiness, and hence of terror and evil. Though whiteness retains its conventional reference, it also becomes a metaphor for the deterministic vision of man "as a helpless creature in a fierce world whose events are determined by forces beyond his control." Stone instances the appeal of a deterministically awesome whiteness for the pre-naturalistic imaginations of Poe and Melville and the post-naturalistic imaginations of Aiken and Frost. Allen traces the course of William James's triumph over a determinism to which he was also willing to give his assent (as in *Principles of Psychology*) in order ultimately to banish it from the moral realm. Allen points up the paradox that "heredity, home environment and early experiences conditioned William James for belief in free will." He demonstrates that James embraced free will out of acute personal necessity and, with the aid of Renouvier, made man's conscious ability to *sustain* a thought an empirical consequence of choice. If human behavior might be said to follow from pre-determined conditions, James argued that moral beliefs determine action and should be counted as one such condition. Allen illuminates the emotional background of James's evolving commitment to "pragmatism" by showing how it originated with his cultivating a belief in free will "as psychiatric therapy" and was strengthened by his introspective studies of volition.

In the third group, Edgar M. Branch and John Lydenberg treat Farrell and Dos Passos, naturalists whose deterministic premises practically begot the need in their heroes to strive for a rebellious freedom; while Sherwood Cummings points out the sources of Twain's determinism and suggests that its severity prevented him from using it in his fiction. Branch demurs from those who relegate Farrell to the bottom of the deterministic sty. He finds freedom to be essential for character development and for the "full pattern of human conduct" in Farrell's fiction. He illustrates how pragmatism and Dewey's ethics inform Farrell's "myth of human liberation." For, however badly off Studs may be materially and emotionally, and however much of a bum he may be, Branch contends that, when regarded from the viewpoint of the moral pragmatists Farrell had read, he is a victim of the habitual in his milieu, and therefore suffers more than anything else from privation of the spirit. Thus, Branch says, "Without the framework of a naturalism that assumes final oblivion for all men, [Farrell] writes about education for life and education for death. He explores growth, self-discovery, creativity—and their frustration." Lydenberg analyzes the implication of Dos Passos's representing "the speech of the people" as vapid clatter. The debasement of the language demonstrates how the popular mind is controlled by the accretion of "official lies disguised as popular truths." Propaganda and advertising become the modern world's contribution to social determinism. Lydenberg also finds that Dos Passos was not "as consistently deterministic as he thinks he wants to be," in that each of the characters he likes "tries to uphold the true meaning of 'old words,' and fights to rebuild ruined words." Their choices of words "are deliberate, and are acts of freedom for which they take the responsibility." Cummings links the black pessimism of Twain's *What is Man?* to his accepting the expansion of Newtonian mechanism into biology, sociology, and eventually into the laws of the mind itself. But, while pointing out that Twain got most of his ideas for this book from Holmes's *Autocrat of the Breakfast Table* and Darwin's *Descent of Man,* Cummings notes that whatever there may be of environmental determinism in his novels comes through more as a means of unfolding thematic ironies than as a conviction about the state of man. Twain's deterministic view of the mind is itself fraught with dualistic ironies. For, machine though it is, the mind "does as it pleases," refuses to obey the commandments of self, and can be improving by training.

It is just possible that the inveterate dualism of that Mark whom Dreiser called the "double Twain" is symptomatic of a national propensity. Whether it is or not, astute analysts of our culture like Henry Adams have significantly associated our instinctive reaction to rigidity with an instinctive dualism. Observing how "from earliest childhood the [New England] boy was accustomed to feel that, for him, life was double," Adams saw the manifestations of this vision in the "instinct of resistance" ("the world [was viewed] chiefly as a thing to be reformed, filled with evil forces to be demolished"), and in the perception that life was shot through with "irreconcilable problems, irreducible opposites."[22] If, in these circumstances, it was inevitable that determinism should hold no mechanistic terrors for American writers, one can understand why our critics should tend to regard determinism as a force that motivates the desire for freedom and makes it worth fighting for. These essays presuppose that the freedom sought by characters in deterministic literature is what makes determinism worth writing about.

NOTES

[1]See Charles C. Walcutt, *American Literary Naturalism, A Divided Stream* (Minneapolis, 1956), pp. 23–29.

[2]Lars Ähnebrink summarizes the familiar "naturalistic" character traits. *The Beginnings of Naturalism in America* (Cambridge, Mass., 1950), p. 28.

[3]Norris made it clear from the beginning that "Vandover's yielding disposition led him to submit to Geary's dictatorship . . .," which ended in his being swindled by Geary, who operated on the idea of "every man for himself." *Vandover and the Brute* (Garden City, New York, 1928), pp. 15f, 220. See also p. 205.

[4]*The Octopus: A Story of California* (Garden City, New York, 1928), II, 343.

[5]Matthew Josephson, *Zola and His Time* (New York, 1928), pp. 530f.

[6]"The Dilemma of Determinism" (1884) in *Essays on Faith and Morals* (New York, 1949), pp. 161f.

7*Image and Idea* (New York, 1949), pp. 128, 137. Originally this essay had appeared in *Partisan Review*, IX (Nov.–Dec., 1942), 483–493.

8*The Financier*, Rev. Ed. (New York, 1927), pp. 134, 414, 392, 443.

9*Jennie Gerhardt* (New York, 1911), p. 93.

10*Ibid.*, p. 132.

11*Rose of Dutcher's Coolly* (New York, 1895), p. 133.

12*Octopus*, II, 106.

13*Ibid.*, p. 344.

14*The Life and Death of The Mayor of Casterbridge* (London, 1920), Wessex Edition, V, 344.

15*Intellectual America: Ideas on the March* (New York, 1941), p. 13. (Cargill is of course well aware of Zola's moralism—pp. 54f.) Ähnebrink, *op. cit.*, p. 26.

16*The Experimental Novel and Other Essays by Emile Zola*, tr. Belle M. Sherman (New York, [1894]), pp. 25f.

17*Sister Carrie* (New York, 1927), p. 83.

18See Robert E. Spiller, *Literary History of the United States*, Rev. Ed. (New York, 1953), p. 1016.

19*American Literary Naturalism*, Ch. VIII (on Dreiser); *Image and Idea*, pp. 131f; *The Beginnings of Naturalism in America*, p. 414; *American Writing in the Twentieth Century* (Cambridge, Mass., 1960), pp. 144f, 180; *Cavalcade of the American Novel* (New York, 1952), pp. 204f; " 'Not Men': A Natural History of American Naturalism," *Kenyon Review*, IX (Summer, 1947), 422, 427; "Frank Norris's Definition of Naturalism," *Modern Fiction Studies*, VIII (Winter, 1962–1963), 409.

20See, *e.g.*, *The Descent of Man*, 1874 (New York, Appleton & Co. [n.d.]), Westminister Edition, IX, 625f.

21*The Pit: A Story of Chicago* (Garden City, New York, 1928), p. 376.

22*The Education of Henry Adams* (New York, 1931), pp. 9, 7.

I

Pre-Naturalistic and
Post-Naturalistic
Determinism

◆LUTHER STEARNS MANSFIELD

Some Patterns from Melville's "Loom of Time"

WHEN HERMAN MELVILLE in 1856 visited his former Berkshire neighbor in Southport, England, Hawthorne recorded a revealing summary of their conversation on the beach:

> Herman Melville, as he always does, began to reason of Providence and futurity, and of everything that lies beyond human ken, and informed me that he had "pretty much made up his mind to be annihilated"; but still he does not seem to rest in that anticipation; and, I think, will never rest until he gets hold of a definite belief. It is strange how he persists—and has persisted ever since I knew him, and probably long before—in wandering to and fro over these deserts, as dismal and monotonous as the sand hills amid which we were sitting. He can neither believe, nor be comfortable in his unbelief; and he is too honest and courageous not to try to do one or the other.

To the man now finding Melville's probing skepticism regrettable, Melville had some six years earlier attributed "that Calvinistic sense of Innate Depravity and Original Sin, from whose visitations, no deeply thinking mind is always and wholly free." And in the next sentence of "Hawthorne and his Mosses" he had offered the explanation: "For, in certain moods, no man can weigh this world, without throwing in something somehow like Original Sin, to strike the uneven balance."

No man could be happy in hearing his friend confess that he had "pretty much made up his mind to be annihilated." But Hawthorne here omitted to observe that this life-long fascination with

19

the problems of freedom and determinism was a significant source of Melville's art. Sometime, in private meditation if not in conversation, Hawthorne himself must have roamed these same dismal and monotonous deserts of philosophy.

Letters, diaries, reports of conversations, marginal pencilings in the books he read, as well as numerous passages in his fictional and poetic works marked the long and tangled trail of Melville's wanderings. But the scholarly mapping of these crossings and recrossings of the desert is not the end. Melville was not an original or systematic philosopher, and lacked the trained habits of thought for that profession. As a man of feeling and an artist, he never accepted the demands for consistency a general formulation would entail, but mused on fate and free will in the more concrete terms of characters and situations. Finally, Ahab must encounter Moby Dick at the Season on the Line: and the reader must meet Melville in his art.

In "The Mat-Maker" chapter of *Moby-Dick,* Ishmael reflected at length on the sword-mat he and Queequeg were weaving:

I was the attendant or page of Queequeg, while busy at the mat. As I kept passing and repassing the filling or woof of marline between the long yarns of the warp, using my own hand for the shuttle, and as Queequeg, standing sideways, ever and anon slid his heavy oaken sword between the threads, and idly looking off upon the water, carelessly and unthinkingly drove home every yarn: I say so strange a dreaminess did there then reign all over the ship and all over the sea, only broken by the intermitting dull sound of the sword, that it seemed as if this were the Loom of Time, and I myself were a shuttle mechanically weaving and weaving away at the Fates. There lay the fixed threads of the warp subject to but one single, ever returning, unchanging vibration, and that vibration merely enough to admit of the crosswise interblending of other threads with its own. This warp seemed necessity; and here, thought I, with my own hand I ply my own shuttle and weave my own destiny into these unalterable threads. Meantime, Queequeg's impulsive, indifferent sword, sometimes hitting the woof slantingly, or crookedly, or strongly, or weakly, as the case might be; and by this difference in the concluding blow producing a corresponding contrast in the final aspect of the completed fabric; this savage's sword, thought I, which thus finally shapes and fashions both warp and woof; this easy, indifferent sword must be chance—aye, chance, free will, and necessity—no wise incompatible—all interweavingly working together. The straight warp of necessity, not to be swerved from its ultimate course—its every alternating vibration, indeed, only tending to that; free will still free to ply her shuttle between given threads; and chance, though restrained in its play within the right lines of necessity, and sideways in its motions directed by free will, though thus prescribed to by both, chance by turns rules either, and has the last featuring blow at events.

As a professional spinner of yarns, Melville sat at just such a Loom of Time. His essential materials, too, were the warp of necessity and the woof of free will. Sailor habits persisting, he continued to use a rough wooden sword like Queequeg's to push the cross strands into place. Indeed, he believed to the end of his life that "Truth uncompromisingly told will always have its ragged edges." But this sensitive and imaginative artisan wove many different patterns.

Working away at his loom, Melville was constantly discovering new qualities in his materials. Some weavers, he learned, tended to confuse necessity and fate, and in *Mardi* Babbalanja helped him to refine his sense of the distinction: "Fatalism presumes express and irrevocable edicts of heaven concerning particular events. Whereas, Necessity holds that all events are naturally linked, and inevitably follow each other, without providential interposition, though by the eternal letting of Providence." The sword continued to give trouble, and he tried different kinds of wood. Perhaps divine providence was a better term than chance, but he was not sure it made a great deal of difference. In any event, all weavers, he found, had trouble with the sword. He was certain there was somewhere a better implement for the purpose. And he hunted along the sandy beach hoping to find a bit of driftwood that would be the right tool. He even gave up weaving for a while to devote full time to the search.

For a narrative artist, precise definitions or inclusive generalizations presented either through his characters or in the author's own right are often less significant than the concrete dramatization of the confrontation of character and event or situation. Thus it seems reasonable to suppose that, for Melville, Tommo in *Typee* represented essentially the free man. Tommo wanted to leave the whaleship and did; later on he wanted to leave the cannibalistic Typees and did. He and Toby felt some anxiety about finding the Happars and eluding the Typees, and at the end of the story, Tommo felt mild remorse about leaving Fayaway and those Typees who had been genuinely friendly, and it was unpleasant for him to have to kill some savages in order to make his escape. But neither the doubt nor the regret was serious enough to deter action. With ingenuity and perhaps a little luck—and only a few minor complications—Tommo could do what he wished, and in Melville's context it would be foolish to think of him as anything but free.

Likewise, because Captain Vere had a choice in the punishment of Billy's homicide, and freely chose between alternatives, the commander of the *Bellipotent* may be regarded as a free man. But Vere was not free in the sense that Tommo was free. For Tommo the alternatives were not attractive: he did not want to stay on the whale-ship or to remain with the Typees. Captain Vere, on the other hand, wanted both to free Billy and to do what he regarded as his duty—and one alternative necessarily ruled out the other. Vere's choice, some critics might argue, was determined by an outside agency, the British naval code, and was thus coercive, whereas Tommo's conduct was inherently his own—call it, perhaps, an instinct of self-preservation. But it was not fear of the navy or any coercive presence of its authority that made Vere go against the advice of his associated naval officers and against his own natural instincts. Rather Vere and Tommo defined themselves differently, and each obeyed his deepest self.

To apply such general terms as fate and freedom in precisely the same way to such different characters and situations would be nonsense. Thus to juxtapose *Typee* and *Billy Budd* may, however, suggest graphically the deepening of Melville's outlook in this philosophical area during the more than forty years intervening between the two books. Chance, free will, and necessity—"all interweavingly working together"—produced more than one pattern on Melville's Loom of Time.

Melville was a belligerent espouser of the supremacy of the self. Nothing Emerson wrote in *Self-Reliance* was foreign to his hope, though he sometimes lacked Emerson's faith. "Whoso would be a man, must be a non-conformist" and "nothing is at last sacred but the integrity of your own mind" were equally articles of Melville's creed. Taji declared in *Mardi* that "the only true infidelity is for a live man to vote himself dead," and Father Mapple's exhortation echoed Emerson powerfully: "Delight is to him—a far, far upward, and inward delight—who against the proud gods and commodores of this earth, ever stands forth his own inexorable self."

The problem, then, for Melville was in the definition of the self. In Ishmael's simple formulation of the controlling elements as chance, free will, and necessity, it may at first have seemed obvious to equate the self and free will. But with increasing maturi-

ty, Melville's profounder view stressed complexity and an inter-
relationship of these elements.

The simpler self of Tommo did not ask questions, nor wonder
how he got an instinct to survive or whether that instinct might
betray his integrity; he was content to get away from his felt
restrictions. That he succeeded meant that he was free. So also
Taji, in *Mardi*, jumped ship to secure his freedom. And he killed
the priest Aleema in a moment of willingness to do whatever was
necessary to release Yillah from captivity. But this apparently free
act of murder lacked the singleness and finality of the departure
from the whale-ship; there were unforeseen consequences in the
loss of Yillah and in Taji's pursuit by the spectre sons of the priest
seeking revenge. Other wills were brought into play, and Taji was
unable to recapture Yillah or to resign himself to do without her
or to accept some substitute satisfaction. His frustration was both
from the outside and from within himself. "Driven from . . .
course, by a blast resistless," he came chartless into "the world
of mind," and though suspicious "that he might only be too bold,
and grope where land was none," he defiantly affirmed that it
was "better to sink in boundless deeps, than float on vulgar shoals."
Taji, that is, was determined to be himself—however that self
might be defined.

In a suggestive and comprehensive way, the same may be
said of Ahab and Pierre. In *Moby-Dick* a natural catastrophe—
a dumb brute's destruction of Ahab's leg—entailed not merely
physical limitations, but psychological consequences as well. In
Pierre the accident (or coincidence) of Pierre's discovery of Isabel
interacted with the traits of his character to determine the future
course of his life. There were differences—particularly in the
nature and number of restrictions laid upon them, in the inci-
dence of fate or necessity, and in their responses to these restrictions—but Taji, Ahab, and Pierre were all romantic heroes bent
on the uninhibited expression of the self.

Beginning with *Mardi* Melville made a wide-ranging but
unsystematic survey of the various kinds of limitation to which
a man's freedom might be subject. Of these restraining or direct-
ing forces, the limited man often had but the vaguest hint; as
Melville said in *Pierre*: "Far as we blind moles can see, man's life
seems but an acting upon mysterious hints; it is somehow hinted

to us, to do thus and thus. For surely no mere mortal who has at all gone down into himself will ever pretend that his slightest thought or act solely originates in his own defined identity."

The progress of Melville's skill at the loom is perhaps more clearly revealed in a suggestive classification of the kinds of limitations variously employed as the warp of necessity or the sword of chance. The early Melville, with many of his contemporaries, commonly accepted the Emersonian idiom in which, since "Nature is the dial-plate of the soul," physical limitation had psychic effects just as psychic states showed outwardly in physical appearance. Hawthorne was a master of the integration of the two levels; thus Chillingworth's acceptance of "a fiend's office" was tallied by his physical decay. Melville used the method with powerful effect to portray Jackson in *Redburn*. Since the influence could operate either way, one kind of limitation slid into another. For Melville, this fusing was likely, since "Nature is not so much her own ever-sweet interpreter," according to his statement in *Pierre*, "as the supplier of that cunning alphabet, whereby selecting and combining as he pleases, each man reads his own peculiar lesson according to his own peculiar mind and mood."

There were, to begin with, the limitations imposed by physical nature, the Not Me, acting outside the physical self. In this category, the unforeseen consequences of an apparently free act were not always clearly to be distinguished from natural catastrophes. Thus, by his own act, Ahab was where he was at the time, when the whale "reaped away [his] leg, as a mower a blade of grass in the field." But in his mind, Moby Dick's dismasting him was not essentially different from the violence of an earthquake; this was nature acting against him from the outside. The congenital stutter of Billy Budd was no less the offense of nature, but it was a part of Billy's physical self, in that he had never known himself without it; it was nature as almost indistinguishable from self. Such gratuitous effects were not always detrimental, for from physical nature also came the personal magnetism that made Ahab a born commander, and Billy Budd was the idealization of the Handsome Sailor. But Melville no less than his characters seemed to take this plus side for granted.

More serious were the limitations that arose from man's social context or from his general connection with human society, as

Ishmael reflected in "The Monkey Rope" chapter on his being tied to Queequeg:

So strongly and metaphysically did I conceive of my situation then, that while earnestly watching his motions, I seemed distinctly to perceive that my own individuality was now merged in a joint stock company of two; that my free will had received a mortal wound; and that another's mistake or misfortune might plunge innocent me into unmerited disaster and death. Therefore, I saw that here was a sort of interregnum in Providence, for its even-handed equity could never have sanctioned so gross an injustice. And yet still further pondering—while I jerked him now and then from between the whale and the ship, which would threaten to jam him—still further pondering, I say, I saw that this situation of mine was the precise situation of every mortal that breathes; only in most cases, he, one way or other, has this Siamese connexion with a plurality of other mortals. If your banker breaks, you snap; if your apothecary by mistake sends you poison, you die.

Ishmael here saw himself as a creditor; but the debtor relationship was equally intolerable to Ahab musing while the carpenter fashioned a new leg:

Here am I, proud as a Greek god, and yet standing debtor to this block-head for a bone to stand on! Cursed be this mortal inter-indebtedness that will not do away with ledgers. I would be free as air; and I'm down in the whole world's books. I am so rich, I could have given bid for bid with the wealthiest Praetorians at the auction of the Roman empire (which was the world's); and yet I owe for the flesh in the tongue I brag with.

For both Ishmael and Ahab, men seemed "detestable as joint stock companies," and it was the single man, in the ideal, who was noble, sparkling, "a grand and glowing creature" with the "august dignity" of the hero. Still, Melville could speak somewhat disparagingly of the crew of the *Pequod* as "*Isolatoes* . . . not acknowledging the common continent of men, but each *Isolato* living on a separate continent of his own." In three different books, nevertheless, he could also hail such a company as "an Anacharsis Clootz deputation," though with perhaps some cynicism about their effectiveness before any judgment bar. Clearly there were times when men should be aware of what Hawthorne called "the magnetic chain of humanity," and the bosom friendship of Ishmael and Queequeg was presented with full sympathy, as were similar relationships in other books. For Melville the balance between a desirable feeling of brotherhood and an indispensable sense of uniqueness was precariously maintained; too much merging in any social context could be damaging to the self.

On the limitations of the single man's freedom which came from the historical past or the cultural heritage, Melville expressed contradictory opinions. On several occasions, most notably in *Mardi,* he saw man as the fortunate heir. "I am full of a thousand souls," Taji joyfully announced, and pictured Homer, Shakespeare, Plato, Zoroaster, and other worthies of the past as converging in him like the various tributaries of the Mississippi, and shaping his thought. Later, there was a fear of "the heavy unmalleable element of mere book-knowledge," and Pierre was censured because "he did not see, that it was nothing at all to him, what other men had written; that though Plato was indeed a transcendently great man in himself, yet Plato must not be transcendently great to him (Pierre), so long as he (Pierre himself) would also do something transcendently great." But, more importantly, the influence of the past was inescapable, not a matter of the individual's choice, and was often deleterious:

Sucked within the Maelstrom, man must go round. Strike at one end the longest conceivable row of billiard balls in close contact, and the furthermost ball will start forth, while all the rest stand still; and yet that last ball was not struck at all. So, through long previous generations, whether of births or thoughts, Fate strikes the present man. Idly he disowns the blow's effect, because he felt no blow, and indeed, received no blow. But Pierre was not arguing Fixed Fate and Free Will, now; Fixed Fate and Free Will were arguing him, and Fixed Fate got the better in the debate.

So Pierre, as the result of whatever antecedent deeds and thoughts —his or his ancestors'—crossed the Rubicon and married his supposed half-sister Isabel. He, like Ahab, would be "free as air," but no man could be.

Besides the limitations of physical nature and those that come from the "joint stock companies" of the social context, past and present, there were the limitations of primarily psychic character, which might merge with limitations of any other sort.

As early as *White-Jacket,* Melville had perceived that "all events are mixed in a fusion indistinguishable," so that what counted ultimately was not the warp or the woof, but the finished mat and its pattern. "What we call Fate" was, to the unsophisticated hero of that volume, "even, heartless, and impartial," and maintained "an armed neutrality." Thus, with over-quick optimism the young sailor concluded: ". . . in our own hearts, we mould the whole world's hereafters; in our hearts, we fashion our own gods. Every mortal casts his vote for whom he will to rule the world. . . . we are precisely what we worship. Ourselves are Fate." The conviction of indistinguishable fusion deepened in Melville, and he returned again and again to the idea that a man is his own fate. He found this conception especially congenial to his temperamental bias for the inviolable self. Stung by Starbuck's rebuke, Ahab was made to meditate, "What's that he said—Ahab beware of Ahab—there's something there!" Yet in other moods Melville doubted the impartiality or neutrality and engaged in what Lawrence Thompson has called his quarrel with God. The *Pequod*'s captain could insist, "Ahab is forever Ahab," and in the same breath explain, "I am the Fates' lieutenant; I act under orders." It was seldom a matter of undiluted joy, even for the man himself, that he had fashioned his own gods and cast a fateful vote.

Like the long-buried vaults of the old Roman halls of Thermes beneath the Hotel de Cluny in Paris, "Ahab's larger, darker, deeper part" was barely hinted on the exterior, but Melville made clear that many of the defining limitations of Ahab arose from undelineated and not precisely measurable forces in his psyche, which, like the sea's most dreaded creatures, were treacherously hidden beneath a calm surface. Ishmael's warning reflected awareness of these psychic terrors: "For as this appalling ocean surrounds the verdant land, so in the soul of man there lies one insular Tahiti, full of peace and joy, but encompassed by all the horrors of the half-known life. God keep thee! Push not off from that isle, thou canst never return." And the warning was echoed in *Pierre*: "Appalling is the soul of a man! Better might one be pushed off into the material spaces beyond the uttermost orbit of our sun, than once feel himself fairly afloat in himself!" Less and less in Melville was outward appearance a reliable index of the soul. Claggart's calm demeanor belied "the tiger heart" within.

The psychic limitation was concretely dramatized in the story of little King Peepi in *Mardi*. According to the lore of Valapee, this infant monarch had inherited the souls of some twenty ancestors—heroes, cowards, sages, simpletons—successively in the ascendant in Peepi. The operation of the cycle made the young king thoroughly unreliable, but Melville defended him: "Thus subject to contrary impulses, over which he had not the faintest control, Peepi was plainly denuded of all moral obligation to virtue. He was no more a free agent than the heart that beat in his bosom." Conflicting souls also victimized Pierre Glendenning in his hope to carry out such contradictory aims as publicly acknowledging Isabel at the same time that he protected his mother from the knowledge of her existence and seeking honorably to conceal his father's secret while he yet made amends to Isabel. In describing Pierre's hopeless predicament, Melville found the moral in *Hamlet* to be "that all meditation is worthless, unless it prompt to action; that it is not for man to stand shillyshallying amid the conflicting invasions of surrounding impulses; that in the earliest instant of conviction, the roused man must strike, and, if possible, with the precision and the force of the lightning-bolt." And Pierre's own perusal of Shakespeare's play, while showing him nothing about the relative wisdom of the "four unitedly impossible designs," did bring an end to his procrastination. He became thenceforward a man of set purpose, however rash or monomaniacal.

When the captain of the *Pequod* asked, "Is Ahab, Ahab? Is it I, God, or who, that lifts this arm?" he forthwith gave his answer: "By heaven, man, we are turned round and round in this world, like yonder windlass, and Fate is the handspike." But Melville suggested a slight variant in his auctorial remarks about Pierre's response to the coincidence that his mother's conversation with the minister about the affair of Ned and Delly answered the question he did not dare ask about her reaction to the revelation of Isabel's parentage: "Strangest feelings, almost supernatural, now stole into Pierre. . . . such coincidences . . . ever fill the finer organization with sensations which transcend all verbal renderings. They take hold of life's subtlest problem. With the lightning's flash, the query is spontaneously propounded—chance, or God?" Ahab seemed certain that God was directly involved; this was fatalism, not necessity, as the terms had been explained by Babbalanja—direct providential interposition. For Pierre, chance and God were not clearly synonymous. In his situation, it could be God acting, or a random force in the universe. When Ishmael named the forces as "chance, free will, and necessity," it is doubt-

ful that he meant to do what Emerson deplored, "to exalt chance
into a divinity" and thus "look too long at the spark." In spite of
occasional outcroppings of Manicheism in Melville's writing, it is
more likely that in the Ishmael passage he was falling back on
his favorite author Solomon, and particularly on Ecclesiastes ix.11:
"I returned and saw under the sun, that the race is not to the
swift, nor the battle to the strong, neither yet bread to the wise,
nor yet riches to men of understanding, nor yet favor to men of
skill: but time and chance happeneth to them all." In the standard
Puritan interpretation of this passage—as in a sermon by Urian
Oakes in 1677—events were "not determined infallibly by the
greatest sufficiency of men or second causes, but by the counsel
and providence of God ordering and governing time and chance
according to His own good pleasure." Melville did not resign himself easily to the opaqueness of the concept, but like Ishmael,
normally accepted the catchall category of chance for aspects of
determinism not otherwise classifiable. He did not go to the length
of Hardy and seriously hypothecate "crass casualty." Indeed, in
certain passages Melville even suggested that the individual man's
freedom was perhaps a limiting factor on divine power, as in
Ahab's defiance of the gods: "Swerve me? ye cannot swerve me,
else ye swerve yourselves! man has ye there. Swerve me? The path
to my fixed purpose is laid on iron rails, whereon my soul is
grooved to run."

Instances of chance were clearest in the final section of *Moby-
Dick*. Though his prophecy had foretold it, it was essentially by
chance that Fedallah was lost on the second day of the chase.
Thus by chance, on the third day, Ishmael, normally in Starbuck's
boat, was selected for the vacancy in Ahab's. It would have been
more normal for one of the harpooners to have replaced Fedallah.
Chance operated further in having Ishmael one of the three sailors
thrown from the boat, but—again by chance—the one not later
restored to his place. Thus Ishmael was left far enough away from
Moby Dick and the sinking *Pequod* not to be menaced by either.
Chance further caused the ravenous sharks to feed elsewhere and
provided the coffin-lifebuoy for him to cling to, so that he was
still alive and afloat when, by chance, the *Rachel* came to his
rescue. Ahab's well-intentioned kindness to Starbuck, in not requir-
ing him to go out in his boat after Moby Dick but leaving him in

the apparently safest spot, aboard the *Pequod,* worked in reverse. In his own more maneuverable boat, Starbuck might have eluded the whale. It was clearly not superior righteousness or moral desert that saved Ishmael. Else why was not Pip saved? If it was Ishmael's feeling of brotherhood toward mankind that saved him, then why was not Queequeg saved? If Ishmael's mental emancipation from Ahab's "fire" view of the world, as recounted in "The Try-Works" chapter, was his claim to salvation, then why did not Starbuck's articulate denouncing of Ahab's purpose save him? Melville intended that chance, not moral merit, had chosen the survivor. Chance had "the last featuring blow at events," but it had been restrained and directed by necessity and free will. And the operation of chance here in no way forestalled the expression of the dominant selfhood of the various characters; rather it provided the occasion for the preeminent quality of each to appear most vividly.

In Melville's final work, *Billy Budd, Sailor,* the focus was not upon Billy and Claggart, as it might have been, but upon Captain Vere. Billy was essentially Ishmael looked at from the outside, a non-voting stockholder in a huge, impersonal joint stock company. To a degree, Claggart was Ahab looked at from the outside, and looked at unsympathetically. He was "depravity according to nature," with no explanation offered of how he got that way. His evil nature must, "like the scorpion for which the Creator alone is responsible, act out to the end the part allotted it." Though not depraved—certainly not in Melville's view—Ahab was also what he was *by nature.* The genesis of his obsessive dedication to the quest for Moby Dick was not explained or dramatized in detail. But the author's inside view presented Ahab, once launched on this quest, as admirably self-reliant and heroic.

Determination and self-reliance were also qualities of Taji, but his life was less tangibly focussed. Indeed, his difficulty was in part his inability to accept Babbalanja's wisdom that "to be, is to be something." He never found what he was willing to settle for. Pierre was ridden by doubts and could call himself, as Ahab never would have, "the fool of Truth, the fool of Virtue, the fool of Fate." He was fascinated by the differences between heavenly and earthly values, hoping perhaps in establishing this distinction to find a way out, a way of excusing his course of action. But there was not in Pierre, as in Starbuck, a dramatic "fall of valor in the soul," a clear failure to act on his best instincts in a specific circumstance. And he experienced nothing comparable to Starbuck's pathetic recognition of his guilt: "I misdoubt me I disobey my God in obeying him." Indeed, Pierre's suicide was dramatic defiance of socially imposed limitations. All three characters were in search of personal identity in the snarled yarns of the Loom of Time. But neither Taji nor Pierre ever achieved Ahab's heroic fidelity nor was vouchsafed his glimpse, while yet cursing "the all-destroying, but unconquering whale," of some possible meaning in the struggle: "Oh, lonely death on lonely life! Oh, now I feel my topmost greatness lies in my topmost grief."

In *Billy Budd*, immediately before presenting Captain Vere, Melville took a digressive "bypath" to idealize his lifelong hero Horatio Nelson as "the greatest sailor since our world began." This was beginning at the top to characterize the type of naval officer Vere represented. He was "an officer mindful of the welfare of his men, but never tolerating an infraction of discipline." In stating that Vere was "intrepid to the verge of temerity," Melville added the qualification "though never injudiciously so." In answering the charge of some detractors that Nelson was guilty of "bravado" and was a "reckless declarer of his person in fight," Melville averred: "Personal prudence, even when dictated by quite other than selfish considerations, surely is no virtue in a military man; while an excessive love of glory, impassioning a less burning impulse, the honest sense of duty, is the first." Like "a true monk" keeping "his vows of monastic obedience," Vere was unwilling to dodge his personal responsibility by waiting to refer Billy's case to the Admiral. This was not love of authority for authority's sake, Melville insisted, but true "self-abnegation." Nelson's dedication to his profession was also given a religious aura, so that on the day of Trafalgar, as Melville saw it, "a sort of priestly motive led him to dress his person in the jewelled vouchers of his own shining deeds." Further, this adornment "for the altar and the sacrifice" was appropriate for the same reason that heroic language was fitting for the literary art that "embodies in verse those exaltations of sentiment that a nature like Nelson, the opportunity given, vitalizes into acts." Vere was a man of intellect and wide reading, which had given him "settled convictions" that served as "a dyke against those invading waters of novel opinion." Not an intransigent conservative, he opposed many of the innovating theories of the day "because they seemed to him insusceptible of embodiment in lasting institutions," and thus "at war with the peace of the world and the true welfare of mankind."

Given these qualities of maturity, intellect, dedication, and courage, Vere was well equipped to exercise such freedom as a man has in the critical moments of definition of himself through conflict. He was like Hawthorne's Arthur Dimmesdale in the preacher's dilemma when forced to choose between the two revered values applicable to his situation: open confession of his sin and active atonement for it. Puritan theology demanded that he both confess and atone, but the law and the social mores of seventeenth-century Boston made these objectives mutually exclusive. If Arthur confessed, the punishment for his crime of adultery might be death, or at the very least banishment or physical mutilation. Granted who he was and what his talents, the most appropriate atonement was the continuance of a devoted and effective ministry. But, not confessing, he was a hypocrite, doomed to a living lie. The turmoil in Dimmesdale's soul arose from his awareness of this fact, at the same time that he saw confession under the circumstances as a species of cowardice, the easy way out, thrusting the matter into the hands of God or chance, much as if Vere had referred Billy's case to the Admiral. As Hawthorne developed the story, the social values of atonement won out with Dimmesdale for seven years, rather than the more theological ones of confession. But Arthur in time saw also the implications of silence: social hypocrisy and lying to one's fellows led inevitably to self-deception and the violation of self-reliance. As Melville developed his story, the social value also won out, promptly and finally, with Captain Vere. Less narrowly defined than Arthur's and of more universal application, Vere's social value went to the very root of the problem of what it is to be a man.

In writing of Pierre's exile and ostracism after his espousal of Isabel's cause, Melville had reflected: "Such, oh thou son of man! are the perils and the miseries thou callest down on thee, when, even in a virtuous cause, thou steppest aside from those arbitrary lines of conduct, by which the common world, however base and dastardly, surrounds thee for thy worldly good." Thirty-five years

later, however, Captain Vere was admirable in Melville's eyes for
fidelity to some of these "arbitrary lines of conduct" and for his
espousal of the idea of such forms in general. He recognized that
the woof of free will served its purpose and got its meaning only
within the framework of the loom.

Facing with equanimity "the clash of military duty with moral
scruple—scruple vitalized by compassion," as Vere explained to
the other members of the court martial, the captain did not act
from impulse, but nonetheless with "the precision and force of the
lightning-bolt," as the moral Melville derived from *Hamlet* would
command. Well aware of the alternatives, but "mindful of para-
mount obligation," he strove "against scruples that may tend to
enervate decision." In accepting their naval commissions, Vere
argued, the officers "in the most important regards ceased to be
natural free agents"; thus "private conscience" must in some instances "yield to that imperial one formulated in the code" of the
navy. This seeming sacrifice of liberty was, however, like the shift
from natural to federal liberty—as Puritan John Winthrop had
defined those terms in his famous speech to the General Court
in 1645—not loss of freedom, but a dedication and implementation
of freedom, in that the church or bride or code, to which one's
pledge was given, was freely chosen. Indeed, this was recognizing,
as Babbalanja put it, that "to be, is to be something"; it was the
replacement of amorphous possibility by concrete actuality. "With
mankind," Captain Vere was repeatedly saying, "forms, measured
forms are everything; and that is the import couched in the story
of Orpheus with his lyre spell-binding the wild denizens of the
woods." This was a plea for civilization, for humanity; for the
differentiation of man from the beast.

In his words to the officers of the court martial, Vere presented the rationale of his action. He saw immediately that the
sole important consideration was the consequence of Billy's act.
He never questioned that there were other forms, perhaps better
forms which amendment, as of the articles of war, might bring
into being. These others were in the realm of maybe; the naval
code was here and now, and it was the form to which he had
dedicated his life. The dedication was as unswerving as Ahab's
under pressure; the captain's own faith in forms was genuine.
Vere was confident that Billy, once he could be made to under-

stand, would approve the sentence. In testimony of some trans-
ference of the captain's faith to the victim came Billy's sincere
valedictory, "God bless Captain Vere!" so convincingly pronounced
that the words awakened in the crew "a resonant sympathetic
echo." The "absence of spasmodic movement" in the hanged body
and "the full rose of the dawn" illuminating the ascending figure
underscored the fact that Billy died at peace with the world.

Significantly Vere's murmured words on his death-bed—"Billy
Budd, Billy Budd"—were "not the accents of remorse." Vere's
mortal wound was received in circumstances similar to Nelson's
death. Vere's spirit of "philosophical austerity" required of himself
the dedication he demanded of others. Thus in these final words
the captain seemed to think of himself as emulating the courage
of the common sailor he had condemned to be hanged, to think
of them both as faithful to a shared sense of "measured forms."

In this final pattern woven, Melville appeared in agreement
with Emerson: "No man has a right perception of any truth, who
has not been reacted on by it, so as to be ready to be its martyr."
For Melville it was this fact that made life tragic and meaningful.
The ball of free will had not dropped from the weaver's shuttle-
hand, but the weaver thought now less of the free unwinding of
the yarn than of where, as woof, the loom would soon imprison
it. Perhaps in a sense different from what the Vivenzan youth had
meant in *Mardi,* it was true that "Freedom is the name for a
thing that is *not* freedom." As Ishmael perceived at the try-works,
"That mortal man who hath more of joy than of sorrow in him,
that mortal man cannot be true—not true, or undeveloped." Probably as early as 1849, Melville had sidelined in his copy of Shakespeare's *King Lear* the affirmation of Edgar:

> Men must endure
> Their going hence, even as their coming hither;
> Ripeness is all.

Courage was a final value for Melville, courage and fidelity.

In the midst of furious action there was serenity in Ahab's
recognition that he had stood forth "his own inexorable self." But
"socially Ahab was inaccessible," a life-long *"Isolato"* in many
respects, though he identified his own woe with "the general rage
and hate felt by his whole race from Adam down." Vere was a
different pattern. He showed no less courage and fidelity; for him

too there was more of sorrow than of joy. His life also came to "ripeness." In their own ways, both Ahab and Vere were as much religious devotees as the old man of Serenia in *Mardi* and might have joined him in saying, "Our lives are our Amens." But acting within a framework of human institutions and critically sensitive to the need for forms, Vere could perhaps feel greater assurance that he acted both for his own integrity and for "the true welfare of mankind." Unlike Ahab, Captain Vere did not seek to be "free as air," but cast his vote to be a man.

◆THOMAS E. CONNOLLY

Fate and "the Agony of Will": Determinism in Some Works of William Faulkner

"THEY WERE doomed, but they lived in the agony of will." This narrative comment by Robert Penn Warren at the end of *All the King's Men* might very well apply to the principal tragic figures of William Faulkner's Yoknapatawpha County. An undergraduate at the University of Virginia came to the heart of the matter with this question addressed to Faulkner: "The role of fate seems very strong in your work. Do you believe in free will for your characters?" Faulkner answered: "I would think I do, yes. But I think that man's free will functions against a Greek background of fate, that he has the free will to choose and the courage, the fortitude to die for his choice, is my conception of man, is why I believe that man will endure. That fate—sometimes fate lets him alone. But he can never depend on that. But he has always the right to free will and we hope the courage to die for his choice"* (38–39 Univ).

*Quotations throughout this paper will be cited in parentheses by page and abbreviated title reference to the following works: *Faulkner in the University,* eds. Frederick L. Gwynn and Joseph L. Blotner (The University of Virginia Press, 1959) (Univ); *Sartoris* (New York: New American Library, 1953) (S); *The Sound and the Fury* (New York: The Modern Library, 1946) (SF); *Light in August* (New York: The Modern Library, 1950) (LA); *Absalom, Absalom!* (New York: The Modern Library, 1951) (AA); "The Bear," *Go Down, Moses* (New York: The Modern Library, 1955) (GDM); *Intruder in the Dust* (New York: The New American Library, 1949) (ID).

Faulkner's novels give evidence that he gradually moved to this position. In the early works, though perhaps vaguely defined, the determining, fatalistic causes of things are stronger than in the later novels in which the victim has more apparent freedom of the will. The form that Fate or determinism takes varies from novel to novel and from character to character throughout Faulkner's works. He described the general condition in answer to a question about Joe Christmas: "I think that you really can't say that any man is good or bad. I grant you there are some exceptions, but man is the victim of himself, or his fellows, or his own nature, or his environment, but no man is good or bad either. He tries to do the best he can within his rights" (118 Univ). To use one of Faulkner's favorite and frequently repeated phrases, ". . . it's man in conflict with his heart, or with his fellows, or with his environment—that's what deserves the pity" (59 Univ).

Sartoris

To begin to trace the determinism in some of Faulkner's fiction, let us look at the novel that Faulkner himself so often recommended that people start with, *Sartoris*. There are two sets of determining forces in this book: one pertains to the whole Sartoris clan and the other applies particularly to young Bayard. The Sartoris family is doomed because it clings to an absurd, outmoded, dead way of life; it clings to the romantic, chivalric, antebellum life of the plantation culture. It is the way of life epitomized by Aunt Jenny's nostalgic reminiscences of having once danced a "valse" with J. E. B. Stuart in Baltimore in '58, and her romanticizing of the self-destruction of the first Bayard during the Civil War anchovy raid: ". . . as she grew older the tale itself grew richer and richer, taking on a mellow splendor like wine; until what had been a hare-brained prank of two heedless and reckless boys wild with their own youth had become a gallant and finely tragical focal point to which the history of the race had been raised from out the old miasmic swamps of spiritual sloth by two angels valiantly fallen and strayed, altering the course of human events and purging the souls of men" (33 S). Old Bayard shows that he still attempts to maintain the antebellum status when he knocks Caspey (who doesn't work for him) through the kitchen door when Caspey refuses to saddle his horse. In a less dramatic way, old Bayard refuses to recognize the change by not financing the purchase of automobiles in his bank. Until Bayard buys a car, his grandfather clings to the horse and carriage which even old Simon recognizes as a sign of the old order. The Sartoris family is doomed to destruction because it cannot change and cope with the new South that emerged from the Civil War. Faulkner, in the voice of the narrator, points out this fact in the chess image on the last page of the novel:

The music went on in the dusk softly; the dusk was peopled with ghosts of glamorous and old disastrous things. And if they were just glamorous enough, there was sure to be a Sartoris in them, and then they were sure to be disastrous. Pawns. But the Player, and the game He plays . . . He must have a name for His pawns, though. But perhaps Sartoris is the game itself—a game outmoded and played with pawns shaped too late and to an old dead pattern, and of which the Player Himself is a little wearied. For there is death in the sound of it, and a glamorous fatality, like silver pennons downrushing at sunset, or a dying fall of horns along the road to Roncevaux. (317 S)

The romantic tone of this comment reveals that, although he was aware of the nature of the family weakness and consequently of the destructive force, Faulkner himself seems, in this early novel, to be, like Aunt Jenny, still enamoured of the old way of life that has passed.

Young Bayard's individual life is determined by a massive guilt complex. Throughout the novel, we are told that he is doomed: "She took his face between her palms and drew it down, but his lips were cold and upon them she tasted fatality and doom . . ." And again, "And they would lie so, holding to one another in the darkness and the temporary abeyance of his despair and the isolation of that doom he could not escape" (247–248 S).

Bayard feels guilty about his brother's death in addition to the psychic shock of the loss of a twin. He also feels guilty about his grandfather's death. Faulkner, himself, gives us the best analysis of the forces that drive young Bayard to seek death. In answer to the question whether young Bayard was not a coward to run away after his grandfather's death, Faulkner replied: "I expect that that one of the twins really wasn't brave and knew it. His dead brother was the braver, I mean capable of that sort of rash recklessness which passes for physical courage. That the one that survived not only had suffered the psychotic injury of having lost a twin, but also he would have to say to himself, The best one of us died, the brave one died, and he no longer wanted to live, actually. He came back home but he probably had no good reason to live . . ." (250 Univ).

Determinism in this early novel is both environmental and psychotic. The family as a whole is doomed because it has not been able to adjust to changes in the social environment. Young Bayard Sartoris is doomed because psychically he cannot survive the death of his twin, and he cannot live with the burden of the guilt he feels for the deaths of both John and his grandfather.

The Sound and the Fury

The Compson family suffers from a defect similar to that of the Sartoris family. When he was asked, "What is the trouble with the Compsons?" Faulkner replied, "They are still living in the attitudes of 1859 or '60" (18 Univ). In The Sound and the Fury, as in Sartoris, two sets of deterministic forces seem to be operating, one with respect to the family as a whole and a different set with respect to the four surviving Compson children.

After a wobbly start in America, the family prospered and reached a peak when it produced a Governor of the State. Then, in the Civil War, a reversal set in, and the family began to decline. General Compson, according to Faulkner, "failed through lack of character" (204 Univ), and it was this failure that, in some unexplained and mysterious way, set the pattern of failure for the whole family.

The action as portrayed by Quentin was transmitted to him through his father. There was a basic failure before that. The grandfather had been a failed brigadier twice in the Civil War. It was the—the basic failure Quentin inherited through his father, or beyond his father. It was a— something had happened somewhere between the first Compson and Quentin. The first Compson was a bold ruthless man who came into Mississippi as a free forester to grasp where and when he could and wanted to, and established what should have been a princely line, and that princely line decayed. (3 Univ)

The Compson family had its origins in a fugitive from Culloden Moor and reached its end in four children of a dipsomaniacal attorney—a suicide, a nymphomaniacal mother of a nymphomaniac, an obsessive-compulsive neurotic, and an idiot. The individuals whose lives are revealed in *The Sound and the Fury* are all victims of individual determining forces over which they have no control. Benjy is the most obvious. As an idiot savant, he can recall without distortion events in the past when he is stimulated by some sensory perception in the present. He exists in an ordered universe, but once the pattern is disturbed, as when Luster drives the horse the wrong way around the statue in the square, he howls in protest. Apart from howling about it, however, Benjy can do nothing, for he is wholly controlled by his environment. The others, Jason III, Quentin, Caddy, Jason IV, and Miss Quentin, though apparently endowed with free will, are, no less than Benjy, controlled by forces over which they have very little control. Mr. Compson, who "sat all day long with a decanter of whiskey and a litter of dogeared Horaces . . ." (8 SF), can do no more to restore the family to its once honorable position than to sell off the last of the Compson land to give Caddy a fine wedding and to send Quentin to Harvard for one year. Quentin is obsessed by a mixture of traits. He sees the family honor resting on his sister's virginity and vainly tries to protect her honor at the same time that he is incestuously attracted to her. Failing to save his sister's virginity, Quentin seeks out his "Little Sister, Death." In committing suicide, Quentin thereby symbolically fulfills the incestuous desire. Shreve asks Quentin, when, on the day of his death, he sees him dressing very carefully, "Is it a wedding or a wake?" (100 SF). When Quentin joins his "Little Sister, Death," it is both a wedding and a wake.

Caddy is as much a victim of her drives as Quentin is of his. At the time of her wedding, she tries to explain to Quentin what it is that causes her sexual promiscuity: "There was something terrible in me sometimes at night I could see it grinning at me I could see it through them grinning at me through their faces . . ." (131 SF). With the exception of Dalton Ames, Caddy does not even love her lovers: ". . . did you love them Caddy did you love them," asks Quentin in anguish, and Caddy answers, "When they touched me I died" (168 SF). Caddy's daughter follows the same path that her mother took, but she lacks Caddy's warmth of heart. The apple, it is said, doesn't fall far from the tree.

Jason, whom Faulkner ironically calls the "first sane Compson since before Culloden" (16 SF), is from childhood driven by a

self-centered Snopesian materialism. Faulkner symbolized this trait
by having Jason keep his hands in his pockets as a child. Speaking of this habit, Faulkner said: "That was a mannerism, keeping
his hands in his pockets, to me that presaged his future, something
of greediness and grasping, selfishness. That he may have kept his
hands in his pocket to guard whatever colored rock that he had
found that was to him, represented the million dollars he would
like to have some day" (263 Univ). Hand in hand with the
materialism in Jason's nature is a hostility toward the world that
expresses itself in acts of cruelty throughout his life, from cutting
up Benjy's dolls as a child to burning the show tickets rather than
letting Luster have one. Of Jason, Faulkner said, "I think that
Jason Compson . . . is completely inhuman. But in a way he is,
I hope, a living man" (132 Univ).

When he was asked whether the de Spain lineage was better
than that of the Compson or the Sartoris families, Faulkner replied: "It was stronger, it was less prone to aberrations, to the
degeneracy into semi-madness which the Compsons reached. It
didn't degenerate into the moral weakness of the Sartorises, it was
tougher blood. It may be it wasn't quite as exalted as theirs was
at one time, that it by instinct—it kept a certain leaven of a
stronger stock by instinctive choice. It was simply stronger—not
better but stronger" (119 Univ).

The Compsons, from General Compson to Miss Quentin, are
relentlessly driven by one form of psychic sickness or another. Jason,
alone, who his mother always insists is a Bascomb, seems with some
success to survive in the Snopesian modern world, and the family
line which started so heroically ends in him, for, though Miss
Quentin may well have children, they will not be Compsons.

Light in August

Joe Christmas, of *Light in August,* is at once most vicious and
most pathetic. In *Sartoris* and in *The Sound and the Fury,* the
characters that were doomed made no real effort to resist their
fate; they merely succumbed. Joe Christmas struggles furiously and
vainly for fifteen years against his fate. In this respect, *Light in
August* marks a turning point in Faulkner's use of determinism.
Because he might have a trace of Negro blood in his veins, society

would classify and stigmatize Joe Christmas. But the more pathetic thing is that Joe, himself, even while resisting the classification, feels guilty about his Negro blood and punishes himself by starting fights in brothels and elsewhere by confessing that he is a Negro. (He anticipates Charles E. St. V. Bon in this respect.) Faulkner felt that Christmas was one of his three "most nearly perfectly tragic" characters:

Now with Christmas, for instance, he didn't know what he was. He knew that he would never know what he was, and his only salvation in order to live with himself was to repudiate mankind, to live outside the human race. And he tried to do that but nobody would let him, the human race itself wouldn't let him. And I don't think he was bad, I think he was tragic. And his tragedy was that he didn't know what he was and would never know, and that to me is the most tragic condition that an individual can have—to not know who he was. (118 Univ)

The first dramatic rejection of Negro blood comes when, at fifteen, Joe violently kicks and punches the young Negro prostitute and then wildly fights with his companions until he is exhausted.

His turn came. He entered the shed. It was dark. At once he was overcome by a terrible haste. There was something in him trying to get out, like when he used to think of toothpaste. But he could not move at once, standing there, smelling the woman, smelling the Negro all at once; enclosed by the womanshenegro and the haste, driven, having to wait until she spoke: . . . He kicked her hard, kicking into and through a choked wail of surprise and fear. She began to scream, he jerking her up, clutching her by the arm, hitting at her with wide, wild blows, striking at the voice perhaps, feeling her flesh anyway, enclosed by the womanshenegro and the haste. (137 LA)

At the end of this episode, Faulkner makes a revealing narrative comment: "He felt like an eagle: hard, sufficient, potent, remorseless, strong. But that passed, though he did not know that, like the eagle, his own flesh as well as all space was still a cage" (140 LA).

In the middle stage of his development, Joe sometimes punishes himself for his Negro blood and once he reverses himself and tries to live as a Negro:

Sometimes he would remember how he had once tricked or teased white men into calling him a Negro in order to fight them, to beat them or be beaten; now he fought the Negro who called him white. He was in the north now, in Chicago and then Detroit. He lived with Negroes, shunning white people. He ate with them, slept with them, belligerent, unpredictable, uncommunicative. He now lived as man and wife with a woman who resembled an ebony carving. At night he would lie in bed beside her, sleepless, beginning to breathe deep and hard. He would do it deliberately, feeling, even watching, his white chest arch deeper and deeper within his ribcage, trying to breathe into himself the dark odor, the dark and inscrutable thinking and being of Negroes, with each suspiration trying to expel from himself the white blood and the white thinking and being. And all the while his nostrils at the odor which he was trying to make his own would whiten and tauten, his whole being writhe and strain with physical outrage and spiritual denial.

He thought that it was loneliness which he was trying to escape and not himself. (196–197 LA)

But the experiment doesn't work. Joe, who is simultaneously a product and a victim of society, must reject the Negro blood and he enters the final stage of his life as a white man. The irony of Joe's condition is that he is never really sure of what he is. When Miss Burden asks him how he can be sure of mixed blood, he answers, "If I'm not, damned if I haven't wasted a lot of time" (223 LA).

As Joe comes close to his catastrophic end, he loses volitional control over his actions. It begins at about nine o'clock on the Friday on which he kills Joanna Burden. He finds that, without being aware, he has wandered into the Negro section of town. The effect of discovering himself surrounded by Negroes is almost destructive:

It was as though he and all other manshaped life about him had been returned to the lightless hot wet primogenitive Female. He began to run, glaring, his teeth glaring, his inbreath cold on his dry teeth and lips, toward the next street lamp. Beneath it a narrow and rutted lane turned and mounted to the parallel street, out of the black hollow. He turned into it running and plunged up the sharp ascent, his heart hammering, and into the higher street. He stopped here, panting, glaring, his heart thudding as if it could not or would not yet believe that the air now was the cold hard air of white people. (100 LA)

Two hours afterward, he finds that, "He was not thinking at all now" (103 LA). And as he moves toward Miss Burden's house, "He didn't think even then *Something is going to happen. Something is going to happen to me*" (103 LA). He is going to murder Joanna Burden, but he expresses it to himself as "Something is going to happen to me." That he has lost control of his will on the verge of murder is clear: "And as he sat in the shadows of the ruined garden . . . he believed with calm paradox that he was the volitionless servant of the fatality in which he believed that he did not believe. He was saying to himself *I had to do it* already in the past tense; *I had to do it. She said so herself"* (244–245 LA).

After the crime, Christmas continues in the same state of suspended will and consciousness. He stops a car and is completely unaware that he has terrorized the young occupants with whom he is riding. It is only after he leaves them that he discovers that he has been holding Miss Burden's pistol in his hand: "The object which had struck him had delivered an appreciable blow; then he discovered that the object was attached to his right hand. Raising the hand, he found that it held the ancient heavy pistol. He did not know that he had it; he did not remember having picked it up at all, nor why. But there it was" (249–250 LA). From this point on, Joe submits more and more to his fate. After a week of running in a circle, Joe is at last ready to accept the place in life to which society has assigned him: when the Negroes start back in frightened recognition as he comes to their cabin, he thinks, "And they were afraid. Of their brother afraid" (293 LA). A few pages earlier, Faulkner used the traded Negro shoes to signal the end of the struggle:

He paused there only long enough to lace up the brogans: the black shoes, the black shoes smelling of Negro. They looked like they had been chopped out of iron ore with a dull axe. Looking down at the harsh, crude, clumsy shapelessness of them, he said "Hah" through his teeth. It seemed to him that he could see himself being hunted by white men at last into the black abyss which had been waiting, trying, for thirty years to drown him and into which now and at last he had actually entered, bearing now upon his ankles the definite and ineradicable gauge of its upward moving. (289 LA)

And once more, at the end of this chapter in which Joe Christmas gives up the struggle against his fate, Faulkner uses the Negro shoes to show that Joe Christmas has finally achieved some form of peace in accepting his fate.

. . . he is entering it again, the street which ran for thirty years. It has made a circle and he is still inside of it. Though during the last seven days he has had no paved street, yet he has travelled farther than in all the thirty years before. And yet he is still inside the circle. "And yet I have been farther in these seven days than in all the thirty years," he thinks. "But I have never got outside that circle. I have never broken out of the ring of what I have already done and cannot ever undo," he thinks quietly, sitting on the seat with planted on the dashboard before him the shoes, the black shoes smelling of Negro: that mark on his ankles the gauge definite and ineradicable of the black tide creeping up his legs, moving from his feet upward as death moves. (296–297 LA)

This is the beginning of the catharsis of the story of Joe Christmas which reaches its fulfillment in Hightower's kitchen. Faulkner describes Joe's death as an apotheosis in terms very similar to those used by Melville when he described the death of another Christ figure, Billy Budd:

For a long moment he looked up at them with peaceful and unfathomable and unbearable eyes. Then his face, body, all, seemed to collapse, to fall in upon itself, and from out the slashed garments about his hips and loins the pent black blood seemed to rush like a released breath. It seemed to rush out of his pale body like the rush of sparks from a rising rocket; upon that black blast the man seemed to rise soaring into their memories forever and ever. They are not to lose it, in whatever peaceful valleys, beside whatever placid and reassuring streams of old age, in the mirroring faces of whatever children they will contemplate old disasters and newer hopes. It will be there, musing, quiet, steadfast, not fading and not particularly threatful, but of itself alone serene, of itself alone triumphant. (407 LA)

Joe Christmas was born into a society that could find a place for him only as a Negro because there was a possibility that he might have had mixed blood. As long as he had a will, he resisted that classification, but eventually he was forced to accept it.

Absalom, Absalom!

Thomas Sutpen, at first blush, would appear to be a man with complete freedom of the will, a man of iron will who has a design and almost brings it off. Sutpen comes very close to fitting exactly Faulkner's definition of man, cited earlier, a man whose "free will functions against a Greek background of fate" (38 Univ). Mr. Compson, in telling his version of Sutpen's story, places him in exactly this position. First he stresses Sutpen's strength and purpose of will: "He was the biggest single landowner and cotton-planter in the county now, attained by the same tactics with which he had built his house—the same single-minded unflagging effort and utter disregard of how his actions which the town could see might look and how the ones which the town could not see must appear to it" (72 AA). And then he places Sutpen against the background of Fate: ". . . he was unaware that his flowering was a forced blooming too and that while he was still playing the scene to the audience, behind him Fate, destiny, retribution, irony—the stage manager, call him what you will—was already striking the set and dragging on the syn-

thetic and spurious shadows and shapes of the next one" (72–73
AA). There is, in the light of this comment, a grim appropriate-
ness in the scythe as the weapon of Sutpen's destruction.

From another point of view Sutpen is depicted as a man
urgently bent on carrying out his design before Fate—the Creditor
—closes the account. Shreve McCannon describes Sutpen as follows: ". . . this Faustus, this demon, this Beelzebub fled hiding
from some momentary flashy glare of his Creditor's outraged face
exasperated beyond all endurance, hiding, scuttling into respect-
ability like a jackal into a rockpile . . . he was not hiding, did
not want to hide, was merely engaged in one final frenzy of evil
and harm-doing before the Creditor overtook him next time for
good and all . . ." (178 AA). Shreve sees Sutpen still at the task
of carrying out his design while trying to avoid his fate when,
after the war, he proposes to Miss Rosa:

> . . . yet before his foot was out of the stirrup he not only set out to try
> to restore his plantation to what it used to be, like maybe he was hoping
> to fool the Creditor by illusion and obfuscation by concealing behind the
> illusion that time had not elapsed and change occurred the fact that he
> was now almost sixty years old, until he could get himself a new batch
> of children to bulwark him, but chose for this purpose the last woman
> on earth he might have hoped to prevail on . . . yet choosing her with a
> kind of outrageous bravado as if a kind of despairing conviction of his irre-
> sistibility or invulnerability were a part of the price he had got for whatever
> it was he had sold the Creditor, since according to the old dame he never
> had had a soul . . . (179–180 AA)

Thomas Sutpen is a continuation of the concept of man that
underlies the character of Joe Christmas. He has greater stature
than Christmas, and he has a plan whereby he hopes to gain
control of his life, his environment. But he is unlike Joe Christmas
in two ways. First, he is less aware of the force that he is fighting;
in fact he is unaware of it. Speaking of his design, Sutpen says to
Quentin's grandfather: "Where did I make a mistake in it, what
did I do or misdo in it, whom or what injure by it to the extent
which this would indicate?" (263 AA). Second, unlike Joe Christmas, Sutpen never accepts what life deals up to him; he never
surrenders his design, but is struck down in full course. Faulkner
has made a very revealing comment about these two qualities in
Sutpen (his failure to realize his mistake and his refusal to deviate
from his design): "To me he is to be pitied, as anyone who
ignores man is to be pitied, who does not believe that he belongs

as a member of a human family, of the human family, is to be pitied. Sutpen didn't believe that. He was Sutpen. He was going to take what he wanted because he was big enough and strong enough, and I think that people like that are destroyed sooner or later, because one has got to belong to the human family, and to take a responsible part in the human family" (80–81 Univ).

Miss Rosa introduces a theme into *Absalom, Absalom!* that anticipates the religious determinism of *The Bear* and represents a third view of determinism in the works of Faulkner. Among the many reasons for her hatred of Sutpen, Miss Rosa is outraged at the fact that he discovered her sister inside a church. She sees both her family and the South as cursed:

In church, mind you, as though there were a fatality and curse on our family and God Himself were seeing to it that it was performed and discharged to the last drop and dreg. Yes, fatality and curse on the South and on our family as though because some ancestor of ours had elected to establish his descent in a land primed for fatality and already cursed with it, even if it had not rather been our family, our father's progenitors, who had incurred the curse long years before and had been coerced by Heaven into establishing itself in the land and the time already cursed. (21 AA)

Faulkner was questioned about this curse on the land during his residence at the University of Virginia:

Q. Mr. Faulkner, throughout your work there seems to be a theme that there's a curse upon the South. I was wondering if you could explain what this curse is and if there is any chance of the South to escape.
A. The curse is slavery, which is an intolerable condition—no man shall be enslaved—and the South has got to work that curse out and it will, if it's let alone. It can't be compelled to do it. It must do it of its own will and desire, which I believe it will do if it's let alone. (79–80 Univ)

Ike McCaslin, as we shall see, takes a very similar position in *The Bear,* and this notion underlies the evolution of Chick Mallison in *Intruder in the Dust.*

The Bear

Ike McCaslin views the South in religious terms. In relinquishing his inheritance, he explains his action to his cousin on two grounds. One is general and applies to the history of the South as a whole, and one is personal and applies to the history of his own family. First of all, he holds that man cannot own the land and consequently cannot buy it or sell it. He bases this notion on the Bible, or rather on his interpretation of it:

Because He told in the Book how He created the earth, made it and looked at it and said it was all right, and then He made man. He made the earth first and peopled it with dumb creatures, and then He created man to be His overseer on the earth and to hold suzerainty over the earth and the animals on it in His name, not to hold for himself and his descendants inviolable title for ever, generation after generation, to the oblongs and squares of the earth, but to hold the earth mutual and intact in the communal anonymity of brotherhood, and all the fee He asked was pity and humility and sufferance and endurance and the sweat of his face for bread. (257 GDM)

The land is tainted, according to Ike, because even before his grandfather bought it, white men had introduced slavery to America, and the particular land that he was repudiating had been tainted because the Indians from whom his grandfather bought it had held slaves on it. He explains to his cousin: "He [God] saw the land already accursed even as Ikkemotubbe and Ikkemotubbe's father old Issetibbeha and old Issetibbeha's fathers too held it, already tainted even before any white man owned it by what Grandfather and his kind, his fathers, had brought into the new land which He had vouchsafed them out of pity and sufferance . . ." (259 GDM).

Ike repudiates his inheritance not only for these generalized reasons, but also because, in the plantation ledgers, he has discovered the history of his own family. His grandfather, apparently without any moral compunction, had fathered a child by one of his slaves, whom he then had married to another slave, and then he had fathered a child by his own slave-child. Ike is horrified by the old man's action of attempting to pay for these wrongs by bequeathing a sum of money to his Negro descendants, "flinging almost contemptuously, as he might a cast-off hat or pair of shoes, the thousand dollars" (269 GDM).

Because of his religious bent, Ike sees himself as a messianic figure, divinely chosen to carry out the work started by his father and Uncle Buddy, who made the first step toward retribution by moving themselves out of and the slaves into the manor house as soon as their father had died. "Maybe He [God] chose Grandfather out of all of them He might have picked. Maybe He knew that Grandfather himself would not serve His purpose because Grandfather was born too soon too, but that Grandfather would have descendants, the right descendants; maybe He had foreseen already the descendants genitive of the three generations He saw it would take to set at least some of His lowly people free—" (259 GDM). To underscore Ike's role of messiah, Faulkner has him purchase a set of carpenter tools when he decides to support himself by his own hands, and says that he does so "not in mere static and hopeful emulation of the Nazarene . . . but . . . because if the Nazarene had found carpentering good for the life and ends He had assumed and elected to serve, it would be all right too for Isaac McCaslin . . ." (309 GDM).

One of the limitations of *The Bear* is that Ike finds only a personal solution to the problem of the curse of the South. He says to McCaslin Edmonds: "I'm trying to explain to the head of my family something which I have got to do which I don't quite understand myself, not in justification of it but to explain it if I can. I could say I don't know why I must do it but that I do know I have got to because I have got myself to have to live with for the rest of my life and all I want is peace to do it in" (288 GDM). It is not until *Intruder in the Dust,* the last of the Yoknapatawpha novels to deal seriously with this socio-moral question, that Faulkner seeks to extend the solution to the South as a whole.

Intruder in the Dust

Chick Mallison, in *Intruder in the Dust,* advances one step beyond Ike McCaslin. He too breaks out of the determining forces of his environment and heritage, but he critically examines his society, initially condemns it, and eventually finds an evolutionary (not revolutionary) solution. The factor that enables Chick to grow or evolve is the same messianic urge that possessed Ike McCaslin, except that in this instance it is politically rather than theologically grounded. The messianic urge, interestingly enough, is a deterministic force over which Chick has very little volitional control.

At the start of the plot, Chick Mallison, a twelve-year-old boy, falls into a creek in winter and is taken by Lucas Beauchamp, a Negro, to his home where his clothes are dried and he is fed what was to have been Lucas's dinner. Chick is a product of his environment. Had a white man treated Chick in the same fashion, Chick would have thanked him and left. But because Chick is a southern white boy and Lucas a Negro, Chick feels obliged to keep the imbalance between the races, and offers to pay Lucas for his hospitality.* Lucas, who insists throughout the novel on being treated not as a member of a particular race but as a human being, refuses the proffered coins and shames Chick. (Lucas's wife, Mollie, would have accepted the coins and thus would have kept the status quo.)

[He] extended the coins: and in the same second in which he knew she would have taken them he knew that only by that one irrevocable second was he forever now too late, forever beyond recall, standing with the slow hot blood as slow as minutes themselves up his neck and face, forever with his dumb hand open and on it the four shameful fragments of milled and minted dross . . . at last it ran to rage so that at least he could bear the shame . . . (14 ID)

Faulkner emphasizes that Chick is a product of his environment immediately after this incident:

. . . he knew that the food had been not just the best Lucas had to offer but all he had to offer; he had gone out there this morning as the guest not of Edmonds but of old Carothers McCaslin's plantation and Lucas knew it when he didn't and so Lucas had beat him, stood straddled in front of the hearth and without even moving his clasped hands from behind his back had taken his own seventy cents and beat him with them, and writhing with impotent fury he was already thinking of the man whom he had never seen but once and that only twelve hours ago, as within the next year he was to learn every white man in that whole section of the country had been thinking about him for years: *We got to make him be a nigger first. He's got to admit he's a nigger. Then maybe we will accept him as he seems to intend to be accepted.* (15 ID)

For months Chick attempts to pay what he considers to be the debt to Lucas by sending gifts to him and to his wife, but Lucas restores matters to their original status by sending back a gift, delivered by a white boy. Finally after three years Lucas fails to recognize Chick in town and the boy feels that he is free at last: *"He didn't even fail to remember me this time. He didn't even know me. He hasn't even bothered to forget me:* thinking in a sort of peace even: *It's over. That was all* because he was free, the man

---

*I am indebted to Professor Dean Doner of Purdue University for this idea of imbalance.

who for three years had obsessed his life waking and sleeping too
had walked out of it" (21 ID).

When Lucas is arrested and charged with murder, Chick's first
impulse is to flee. Several times he thinks that he will get on his
horse, Highboy and ride as far as he can away from Lucas, but the
subconscious messianic urge causes him to "forget" to prepare the
horse for the journey:

> —and he remembered again that he had forgot to give Highboy the extra
> feed this morning too but it was too late now and besides he was going to
> carry feed with him anyway—he knew exactly what he was going to do:
> . . . he would go home and saddle Highboy and tie a sack of feed behind
> the saddle and turn him in a straight line in the opposite direction . . .
> and ride in that one undeviable direction . . . at last all over finished done,
> no more fury and outrage to have to lie in bed with like trying to put your-
> self to sleep counting sheep . . . (32–33 ID)

Despite this urge to flee, Chick cannot leave, for he must give
Lucas a final chance to call up the debt: ". . . he said *What the
hell am I doing here* then answered himself the obvious answer:
not to see Lucas, he had seen Lucas but so that Lucas could see
him again if he so wished . . ." (33 ID).

When Lucas asks Chick to dig up the grave to prove his
innocence, Chick instantly recognizes his role:

> So he wasn't listening, not even to his own voice in amazed incredulous
> outrage: "Me go out there and dig up that grave?" He wasn't even think-
> ing anymore *So this is what that plate of meat and greens is going to cost
> me.* Because he had already passed that long ago when that something—
> whatever it was—had held him here five minutes ago looking back across
> the vast, the almost insuperable chasm between him and the old Negro
> murderer and saw, heard Lucas saying something to him not because he
> was himself, Charles Mallison junior, nor because he had eaten the plate of
> greens and warmed himself at the fire, but because he alone of all the
> white people Lucas would have a chance to speak to between now and
> the moment when he might be dragged out of the cell and down the steps
> at the end of a rope, would hear the mute unhoping urgency of the eyes.
> (53–54 ID)

(It might be noticed that it is at this point in the novel, after 54
pages, that the reader learns Chick's full name. Only when he accepts his role as savior does Chick gain his complete identity.) From
this point on, Faulkner extends the relationship between Chick and
Lucas to the whole southern white-Negro relationship. By extension,
Chick's personal debt to Lucas becomes the debt that the South

owes to the Negro race, and the thesis of the novel is that the South, like Chick, will have to face the Negroes and pay off the debt.

Intruder in the Dust is at the opposite swing of the pendulum from *Sartoris,* in which a family inflexibly clings to an outmoded way of life and this leads to individual moral paralysis. Chick Mallison has reached the point at which the individual can rise above the culture and heritage into which he has been born, and act according to the dictates of his own conscience to oppose that way of life. His uncle, Gavin Stevens, phrases what Chick has discovered: "Some things you must never stop refusing to bear. Injustice and outrage and dishonor and shame. No matter how young you are or how old you have got. Not for kudos and not for cash: your picture in the paper nor money in the bank either. Just refuse to bear them. That it?" (157 ID).

In the twenty years between *Sartoris* and *Intruder in the Dust,* Faulkner's view of life shifted from a heavy emphasis on determinism to a stress on man's ability individually to exercise a measure of control. But it is the special man who does it, not necessarily every man. The last two questions in *Faulkner in the University* are a fitting conclusion to this study of determinism in a selection of Faulkner's fiction:

Q. Sir, it means that your basic conception of life is optimistic?
A. Yes.
Q. But not of the individual.
A. Well, the individual is not too much, he's only a pinch of dust, he won't be here very long anyway, but his species, his dreams, they go on. There's always somebody that will keep on creating the Bach and the Shakespeare as long as man keeps on producing.

II

Symbolic and
Philosophic
Considerations

◆EDWARD STONE

The Devil Is White

JUST AS there has always been a symbolism of flowers in literature (a brief discourse on which we get from the mad Ophelia),
so there has been one of colors. While certain color associations are
persistent and predictable, others are surprising; and if most often
they are both, it may be because, like lovers, colors seem to speak
in two voices at the same time.

Green, for example, as far back as the fourteenth century,
symbolized not only coolness and verdure but also the devil in
disguise, as a mimicry, for that oldest of all hunters in green
forests.[1] And although Goethe found in green only "a distinctly
grateful impression" ("the beholder has neither the wish nor the
power to imagine a state beyond it") and categorically divides colors
into those "on the plus side" (yellow, orange, and minimum cinna-
bar) in that "the feelings they excite are quick, lively, aspiring"
and those "on the minus side" (blue, red-blue, and blue-red) in
that "they produce a restless, susceptible, anxious expression,"—still
he conceded the possibility of qualified or even opposing reaction.
By only a "slight and scarcely perceptible change," Goethe found
that the effect on the spirit of yellow, that "colour of honour and
joy" is "reversed to that of ignominy and aversion"; conversely,
although in its darker hues red "conveys an impression of gravity
and dignity," in its lighter tints its impression is one "of grace and
attractiveness"; "and thus the dignity of age and the amiableness of
youth may adorn itself with degrees of the same hue."[2]

Now this same enigmatic ability of the color white to evoke two opposing feelings had been noted early and in a facetious context by Rabelais in the sixteenth century. In *Gargantua* (Book I, Chapter 9) he invests Gargantua with the colors of blue and white, the white expressing "joy, pleasure, delight, and rejoicing"; then extends his essay on "this symbolic use of colors" into the next chapter, finding data in pagan and biblical times, yet introducing—even if only to refute it—the ancient argument that white also has a mysteriously *terrifying* effect as well: ". . . 'why does a lion, whose roar terrifies all animals, fear and respect only the white rooster?' "

Succeeding centuries have not found an answer to this "insoluble" problem as jubilantly satisfying as Rabelais's. Indeed, in the past century there has been a gradual yielding in importance of the symbolic meaning of white to the rare meaning that had puzzled that forgotten contemporary of Marcus Aurelius's: increasingly white appears in the literature of western man as the color of terror and despair. It would seem that, despite (because of?) our intellectual sophistication, the devil has not disappeared at all: he has simply changed identity and, with it, color. This trend has apparently also been one from faith to a despair consonant with a deterministic view of the universe.

It is true that we can observe the traditional concept of white as purity, as celestial radiance (immortality of death), always functioning in American literature. In 1689 we find Cotton Mather telling his readers, "There is mention of creatures that they call *White witches,* which do only Good-Turns for their Neighbors," yet only to reject the phrase as a contradiction in terms: "I suspect," he continues, "that there are none of that sort . . ."[3] To him white would without question always be the color of faith. And Professor Harry Levin has reminded us that in Jonathan Edwards' *Images, or Shadows of Divine Things,* "Since holiness comprehends all the other virtues, it is typified by white, which is also the type of purity because it signifies mothers' milk and childish innocence."[4]

Yet white means no less as late as the 1920s in *The Great Gatsby.* Moreover, even Fitzgerald's more famous contemporary, Ernest Hemingway, as deterministic a writer as Fitzgerald is not, occasionally associates white with pleasant or even inspiring thoughts.

Other examples of idealistic symbolic use of white mark our literature at every step between these dates. We are not surprised to find it characteristic of the writers of New England. The Thoreau who can speak (in the "Solitude" chapter of *Walden*) of the "indescribable innocence and beneficence of Nature—of sun and wind and rain, of summer and winter," predictably finds that

it is a surprising and memorable, as well as valuable experience, to be lost in the woods any time. Often in a snow-storm, even by day, one will come out upon a well-known road and yet find it impossible to tell which way leads to the village. Though he knows that he has travelled it a thousand times, he cannot recognize a feature of it, but it is as strange to him as if it were a road in Siberia. . . . Every man has to learn the points of compass again as often as he awakes, whether from sleep or any abstraction. Not till we are lost, in other words not till we have lost the world, do we begin to find ourselves, and realize where we are and the infinite extent of our relations.

Similarly, the Emerson of "The American Scholar" who believed that "Nature is the opposite of the soul, answering it part for part. . . . Its beauty is the beauty of his own mind. Its laws are the laws of his own mind"—this Emerson looks upon the snow as an equally blessed phenomenon. In "The Snow-Storm" he calls the snow a "fierce artificer": it may be *myriad-handed, wild, fanciful, savage,* and *mocking,* yet more than all else it is an artist whose natural effects are striking enough to make human art gape in admiration. And this, again, is essentially the snow of Whittier's "Snow-Bound"—a phenomenon of "starry flake and pellicle" creating a "glistening wonder," creating "marvellous shapes" and furnishing a whiteness that though violent is one that man easily (and cosily) protects himself against by the effort of his own hands; for "Snow-Bound" is predominantly the testament of an unquestioning faith in a God who watches the fall of every sparrow. In Emily Dickinson, as we shall see, white calls forth a variety of responses. Certainly she could think, in looking at children's graves, of "Sparrows unnoticed by the Father"; "Lambs for whom time had not a fold"; yet usually with her, white is the white of purity and heavenliness. Even with Hawthorne, no great variation is observed from this way of thinking of white. It is true that the view (in Chapter 5 of *The Blithedale Romance*) of the surrounding countryside that the feverish Coverdale has from his cold bedroom window during his first night at Blithedale is a chilling one ("the moon was shining on the snowy landscape, which looked like a lifeless copy of the world in marble"), but we remember his physical condition. And in any event, the vision is quickly forgotten, steadfast as Hawthorne's faith was. In *The House of the Seven Gables* (Chapter 2) he pauses to reflect that "life is made up of marble and mud. And, without all the deeper trust in a comprehensive sympathy above us, we might hence be led to suspect the insult of a sneer, as well as an immitigible frown, on the iron countenance of fate. What is called poetic insight is the gift of discerning, in this sphere of strangely mingled elements, the beauty and the majesty which are compelled to assume a garb so sordid." In *The Blithedale Romance* he again entertains the idea of the indifference of a deterministic universe only to reject it. Even if Nature is as "well pleased" with the "ranker vegetation" that grew from Zenobia's corpse as it was with "all the beauty" of Zenobia alive, this in no way weakens his "deeper trust" in God's providence: "It is because the spirit is inestimable that the lifeless body is so little valued" (Chapter 28). The beauty and majesty that Hawthorne speaks of are exemplified in the white roses that Phoebe Pyncheon decorates her gloomy, history-crammed bedroom with: by subtle suggestion these transform it into a maiden's bedroom again—that is, purify it, associate it with virginity. And, of course, there is the excessive symbolic employment of white in *The Marble Faun*, where Hilda's white doves are meant to represent her purity and at the close of which Kenyon speaks of her "white wisdom . . . as a celestial garment." Similarly, in Longfellow's "Cross of Snow" the cross is a whiteness of immortality and of the beloved dead wife of whom the poet says "soul more white never through martyrdom of fire was led to its repose."

So, too, with the regional literature of our country, it would seem. In Bret Harte's story of 1869, the outcasts of Poker Flat voice no complaint against the snow that finally reaches twenty feet in depth; and although it causes their death, it emerges as a benevolent agent of the universe: "Feathery drifts of snow . . . settled about them as they slept. . . . all human stain, all trace of earthly travail, was hidden beneath the spotless mantle mercifully flung from above."

Yet during the same century this faith was undergoing a weakening, even a shock; and with this change the literary record undergoes a corresponding change. We observe that now and then it is possible to detect a mixture of both faith and doubt in the same writer. The snow of Longfellow's "Snow-Flakes" for once is not raging or violent, yet is the more upsetting for its calm. Here whiteness expresses actual despair, whether in the white face of the human "troubled heart" or the "secret of despair"

> Long in its cloudy bosom hoarded,
> Now whispered and revealed
> To wood and field.

And of Emily Dickinson's familiar metaphor

> Death is the other way—
> . . . .
> It—is the White Exploit—

Professor Charles Anderson is moved to comment: "She never found a better image for its ambiguity than this, man's bold adventure into blankness. Death or immortality?"[5]

Increasingly it begins to seem that this may not be my father's world at all, but his infernal antagonist's. How pronounced becomes the wavering of faith, then tendency to associate whiteness with an anti-religious concept of the universe; and, whether by statement or implication, with man as a helpless creature in a fierce world whose events are determined by forces beyond his control! This tendency, which has never been absent from our literature and which slowly threatens to dominate it as a symbolic force, would seem to go back at least as far as Edgar Allan Poe. Half a century ago Henry James might insist that in *The Narrative of Arthur Gordon Pym* "There *are* no connexions; not only . . . in the sense of further statement, but of our own further relation to the elements, which hang in the void; whereby we see the effect lost, the imaginative effort wasted";[6] but recent criticism of the "horrific" with which *Pym* ends has called attention to the significance of this section from a metaphysical point of view, in particular, the studies of Professors Edward Davidson and Charles O'Donnell.

Nor need we limit ourselves to *Pym*. With Poe whiteness conveys terror, whether aesthetically or metaphysically. Commenting on Roderick Usher's paintings, the narrator cites as "one of the phantasmagoric conceptions" a picture of a long white tunnel with no outlets which Usher had bathed with "a flood of intense rays . . . in a ghastly and inappropriate splendour." Similarly, in the first paragraph of "The Pit and the Pendulum" the seven white candles on the table of the Inquisition tribunal appall and almost nauseate the condemned narrator. But the most telling is the evidence of "Berenice." Its morbid hero, musing too long on "the alteration" in Berenice's teeth, confesses that "I shuddered as I assigned to them in imagination a sensitive and sentient power, and even when unassisted by the lips, a capability of moral expression." Thus does he divest God of any identity other than as the creator of force.

Other writers were to follow him. The ambiguity that Professor Anderson says characterizes Dickinson's image of death, for example, vanishes, and the whiteness at least once emerges as basically nothing less than the color of a deterministic universe:

> Apparently with no surprise
> To any happy flower,
> The frost beheads it at its play
> In accidental power.
>
> The blond assassin passes on,
> The sun proceeds unmoved
> To measure off another day
> For an approving God.

And there is the prominent example of Herman Melville. What may we predict about a man who insists that "though in many of its aspects this visible world seems formed in love, the invisible spheres were formed in fright"? Who speaks of life as "a vast practical joke"; says of the Pequod's crew that "we . . . blindly plunged like fate into the lone Atlantic", and from a contemplation of Pip's fate concludes that "man's insanity is heaven's sense; and wandering from all mortal reason, man comes at last to that celestial thought, which, to reason, is absurd and frantic; and weal or woe, feels then uncompromised, indifferent as his God"? The answer is in the "Whiteness of the Whale" chapter of *Moby-Dick,* where the book is baptised, it will be recalled, *in nomine d——*. Here (in a passage borrowed largely from Rabelais, as it happens) he speaks of a "dumb blankness, full of meaning, in a wide landscape of snows— a colorless all-color of atheism from which we shrink." This is merely one of a number of instances of passages of this sort. We remember his inability to decide why white "appeals with such

power to the soul; and more strange and far more portentous—
why . . . it is at once the most meaning symbol of spiritual things,
nay, the very veil of the Christian's Deity; and yet should be as it
is, the intensifying agent in things the most appalling to mankind."
We should remember too that other great shock to Ishmael's soul,
the giant white squid: "A vast pulpy mass, furlongs in length and
breadth, of a glancing cream-color, lay floating on the water,
innumerable long arms radiating from its centre, and curling and
twisting like a nest of anacondas, as if blindly to clutch at any
hapless object within reach. No perceptible face or front did it
have; no conceivable token of either sensation or instinct; but
undulated there on the billows, an unearthly, formless, chance-like
apparition of life" (Chapter 59). And it is hard in reading Melville's "dream" poem "The Berg" not to feel that the walls whose
"dead indifference" he shudders at are not those of an iceberg but
those of God.

This "iconology of whiteness, pondered over by Melville,"
Professor Harry Levine writes, "has furnished one of the farthest
ranging chapters in our literature."[7] Indeed, the very snow that
Thoreau and Emerson thrilled at has also undergone a striking
change in this function as "symbol of spiritual things." Would it
not prove an engaging adventure in ideas to contrast Thoreau's
reaction to being lost in a snowstorm with that of Hans Castorp
in *The Magic Mountain* or to note the frightening transformation
of Bret Harte's sentimental blanket of snow into James Joyce's mantle of death and despair in "The Dead." But our own literature
yields evidence enough. There is Stephen Crane's crazed and drunk-
en Swede emerging from the blue hotel into a raging whiteness:
"He might have been in a deserted village. . . . here, with the
bugles of the tempest pealing, it was hard to imagine a peopled
earth. One viewed the existence of man then as a marvel, and
conceded a glamor of wonder to these lice which were caused to
cling to a whirling, fire-smitten, ice-locked, disease-stricken, space-
lost bulb. The conceit of man was explained by this storm to be
the very engine of life. One was a coxcomb not to die in it." The
conceit in question being, of course, man's ancient trust in the
dignity of man, of the divine gift of reason, and in the sentience
of his creator. Not many minutes afterwards the Swede does die,
at the hands of a gambler with a knife that shoots forward to the

end that "a human body, this citadel of virtue, wisdom, power, was pierced as easily as if it had been a melon." Such savagery of deterministic metaphor would be hard to equal.

Yet as we move into the present century we notice that the trend continues and even its intensity is unabated. Crane's successor, Jack London, equals it in "The White Silence." What importance do the two men and Indian woman have in his eyes as he watches them trudge along behind their savage dogs in the snow?

The afternoon wore on, and with the awe, born of the White Silence, the voiceless travelers bent to their work. Nature has many tricks wherewith she convinces man of his finity—the ceaseless flow of the tides, the fury of the storm, the shock of the earthquake, the long roll of heaven's artillery—but the most tremendous, the most stupefying of all, is the passive phase of the White Silence. All movement ceases, the sky clears, the heavens are as brass; the slightest whisper seems sacrilege, and man becomes timid, affrighted at the sound of his own voice. Sole speck of life journeying across the ghostly wastes of a dead world, he trembles at this audacity, realizes that his is a maggot's life, nothing more. Strange thoughts arise unsummoned, and the mystery of all things strives for utterance.

This is man as cipher, as member of the animal creation, and struggling for mere existence on Darwinian terms:

Bursting into the camp, he saw the girl in the midst of the snarling pack, laying about her with an ax. The dogs had broken the iron rule of their masters and were rushing the grub. He joined issue with the butt of his rifle, and the hoary game of natural selection was played out with all the ruthlessness of its primeval environment.

To Henry Adams, the intellectual, Darwinism had also been an object of contemplation, and of a far more comprehensive kind. In it he could find merely a scientific substitute for religious faith, yet one less satisfactory than religion even, teleologically speaking. Incapable of faith by now, he was doomed to helpless despair the first time deep personal loss overtook him, which happened in the summer of 1870. Summoned from London to the Italian bedside of his sister, who was dying an excruciatingly painful death from lockjaw resulting from a cab accident,—we read in Chapter 19 of *The Education,* fittingly entitled "Chaos",—he perceives that of all the Italian summers he has known, this is the most "winning" physically, and he must redefine his understanding of Nature's position with regard to human mortality. "Nature enjoyed it, played with it, . . . she liked the torture . . .," he muses grimly with "violent emotion." Although he had known death before, it was all as nothing. Now he knows. "The first serious consciousness of Nature's gesture—her attitude towards life—took form then as a phantasm, a nightmare, an insanity of force. For the first time, . . . the human mind felt itself stripped naked, vibrating in a void of shapeless energies. . . . Society became fantastic, a vision of pantomime with a mechanical motion . . ." Gone then is his ability to believe in "any personal deity," and travelling north from the terrible scene, he makes a shocking discovery: "For the first time in his life, Mont Blanc for a moment looked to him what it was—a chaos of anarchic and purposeless forces—and he neded days of repose to see it clothe itself again with the illusions of his senses, the white purity of its snows, the splendor of its light, and the infinity of its heavenly peace."

In the company of these twentieth-century reflections we may place the poet Conrad Aiken. Remembering his "Silent Snow, Secret Snow" and his "Mr. Arcularis," we incline to agree with John Updike, who concludes from Aiken's short stories that "the cosmic vacuity, the central *nihil* haunts him; 'the great white light of annihilation' illuminates his scenes and to an extent bleaches them."[8] That this bleaching whiteness is in truth the color of his deterministic view of the universe, we learn directly from Aiken's own artist Demarest in *Blue Voyage* (1927), who speaks both for himself and his generation:

[I am always] producing in the end not so much a unitary work of art as a melancholy *cauchemar* of ghosts and voices, a phantasmagoric world of disordered colours and sounds; a world without design or purpose; and perceptible only in terms of the prolix and the fragmentary . . . but . . . I have deliberately aimed at this effect, in the belief that the old unities and simplicities will not longer serve . . . if one is trying to translate, in any form of literary art, the consciousness of modern man. And this is what I have tried to do.

Now just such a world, expressed in just such terms, is the world of the great modern poet Robert Frost. "A terrifying poet," Lionel Trilling called him: "The universe that he conceives is a terrifying universe. Read the poem called 'Design' and see if you sleep the better for it."[9] The color of that universe is consistently white. The "self-same Power" that once led Emerson to the Rhodora's soul-satisfying feast of color (the purple petals afloat on black water, with the red of a bird possibly blending in) is now likely to lead Frost, if not simply in circles, then into a chamber of equally natural horrors. "Design" is merely the most frightening (and for this reason, perhaps the least typical) of Frost's expressions of distaste, of disbelief in providence—its heaped-up whiteness of spider, moth, and cloth-likeness, on a flower ordinarily blue but here white inviting the question of "Why?" and evoking the shuddering question-answer of

> What but design of darkness to appall?—
> If design govern in a thing so small.

Is this not the piety of Gerard Manley Hopkins in reverse? As that poet had praised Him for the Design of Daylight, for Pied Beauty; so now the midnight poet denies Him for Blank Horror, for the Design of Darkness with its absence of "All things counter, original, spare, strange." Design did indeed "govern in a thing so small" back in the devout seventeenth-century world of Edward Taylor, whose spider had also been the devil but one whose whipcord tangles a "mighty, gracious Lord" could give man grace enough to break; and in the eighteenth-century world of Jonathan Edwards, who could observe the wondrous way of the working of the spider with "wonderment and pleasure," confident that the spider's self-destruction was planned by the same power that, he noted, left spider eggs behind for "a new stock the next year."

Elsewhere again and again Frost answers his question in a way that we would expect, for it is no question but, like Melville's an answer. And typically this determinism reveals itself in his reflections on the whiteness, not of aesthetically repulsive night-time objects at all, but of the traditional natural phenomena of God's world.

To the buoyantly confident Emerson, a man for whom, unlike Dickinson, "Nature never wears a mean appearance," the Emerson of *Nature* with its description of the stars as "envoys of beauty" that "light the universe with their admonishing smile," Robert Frost rises in life-long opposition. Just how grim twentieth-century man might find those very stars we had had a foreshadowing of in the closing years of the preceding century: in Stephen Crane's "Open Boat," with its despairing correspondent kneeling in supplication to the nighttime heavens and observing: "A high cold star on a winter's night is the word he feels that she says to him. Thereafter he knows the pathos of his situation." As does the humble questioner of Frost's early, obscure "Stars" (in *A Boy's Will,* 1913). He too begins with a wondering, a musing "How countlessly they congregate . . . As if with keenness for our fate," but ends with a recognition of their inexorability (and his own helplessness) :

> And yet with neither love nor hate,
> Those stars like some snow-white
> Minerva's snow-white marble eyes
> Without the gift of sight.

But more than all else,—snow. And for all that whiteness is capable of inspiring thoughts other than dread to him (wherein he differs from Poe), still it is this aspect that most frequently daunts his faith. To be sure, in "Stars" the snow appears simply at first as "tumultuous," as that

> Which flows in shapes as tall as trees
> When wintry winds do blow!

and yet in the next breath death appears as "white rest, and a place of rest/Invisible at dawn." And although we have the evidence of "The Onset" that contemplation of a snowstorm can inspire affirmation in Frost—

> I know that winter death has never tried
> The earth but it has failed . . .
> . . . .
> And I shall see the snow all go down hill
> In water of a slender April rill.
> . . . .
> Nothing will be left white but here a birch
> And there a clump of houses with a church

—still the brief if striking piety of that last phrase is effectively devastated by the reflections of one of his most engrossing (and familiar) poems, "Desert Places." For *desert,* of course, we are asked to read *empty,* devoid of meaning. Nothing less than this is the modern man's Minerva, goddess of wisdom. Even the findings of the New Science of astronomy are of no great concern to him (no more than they had been to Donne or to Pascal) ; yet this is because the creation closer up, the empirically real creation, is so much *more* spiritually annihilating. He is speaking of the snow falling about him. It is whiteness frightening in its ability to cancel out all evidence of man's work and will, all contours and designs, all relationships of objects to each other without which we have no importance. And we are at a time when night is merely falling, when the ground is not quite effaced in whiteness. When night takes over completely, alas, we shall see nature at her worst. Then there will be nothing but an undifferentiated whiteness against a total darkness—a stark contrast of pure white and pure black full of soundless fury ("no expression") and signifying nothing ("nothing to express"). *These* are the truly frightening desert places, then —the ones "so much nearer home": they mirror and reaffirm the poet's prior intimations of doubt and despair at his helplessness.

And I think that the foregoing examples, random though they are, in their aggregate suggest to us that these are more and more the desert places of the American writer. To him the devil is as real as to Cotton Mather, for all that in his infinite resourcefulness he has put on a costume of a different color. When the next "damp, drizzly November" smothers the soul of our Ishmael, when his "hypos" get "the upper hand" of him, will he again "quietly take to the ship"—he who has found "coffin warehouses" at sea far more frightening than any in his confining "insular city of manhattoes?" Verily, the prince of darkness now insolently sails all seven of the seas, resplendent in the white radiance once reserved for eternity.

NOTES

[1] D. W. Robertson, Jr., "Why the Devil Wears Green," *Modern Language Notes,* LXIX (November, 1954), 470–472.

[2] *Farbenlehre (Theory of Colors),* Charles Eastlake translation (London, 1840).

[3] "A Discourse on Witchcraft," in *Memorable Providences,* etc. (Boston, 1689).

[4] *The Power of Blackness* (New York, 1958), p. 32.

[5] *Emily Dickinson's Poetry* (New York, 1962), p. 227.

[6] *The Novels and Tales of Henry James* (New York, 1907–1909), Preface, Vol. XVII.

[7] *The Power of Blackness,* p. 28.

[8] *The New Republic,* CXLIII (November 28, 1960), 26.

[9] "A Speech on Robert Frost," *Partisan Review,* XXVI (Summer, 1959), 451.

⚘GAY WILSON ALLEN

William James's
Determined Free Will

THE PUN in my title is more serious than witty. The most outright determinist could easily find many factors in William James's ancestry, physiology, mind, and personal experiences that caused him to seek and espouse free will. His father, Henry James Senior, revolted against his Calvinistic father, and devoted much of his life to cultivating "spontaneity" in his children.[1] As a consequence his oldest son, William, received so undisciplined an education that he grew up with the conviction that as a scientist and scholar he was severely handicapped. But whether handicapped or not, heredity, home environment, and early experiences conditioned William James for belief in free will.

And he was also conditioned by psychological pressures. Probably James's will-power was never as weak as he thought it was in his early twenties, when he became so neurotic that he repeatedly contemplated suicide.[2] At that time the problem of determinism versus free will was so personal and threatening to him that he literally embraced the doctrine of free will to save his life, and his rationalizing of his choice lies at the root of his voluminous writings on psychology and philosophy. For example, his chapter on the Will in *Principles of Psychology* is almost straight autobiography. This relationship between James's life and writings is, of course, the proper subject for biography (on which I am currently engaged), but the biographical background is so important in his theories of the Will that I must at least indicate the origin and order of his thinking on the subject.

In 1867 James interrupted his medical studies at Harvard to spend a year in Germany, ostensibly to study empirical science, but secretly to find a cure for enervating pains in his back, for which the medical science of the day could discover no organic cause. In Germany he found no cure for his mysterious illness, and his assiduous reading of such pessimists as Schopenhauer and such determinists as Herbert Spencer aggravated his neurotic condition. Then the death of his cousin Minny Temple, in the spring of 1870, was fully as traumatic in his own life as in his brother Henry's. In his diary he wrote, "By that big part of me that's in the tomb with you, may I realize and believe in the immediacy of death!" He resolved to "ascend to some sort of partnership with fate . . ."[3]

But a week later he felt less fatalistic and wrote in his diary: "I think that yesterday [April 29] was a crisis in my life. I finished the first part of Renouvier's 2nd Essay and saw no reason why his definition of free-will—the sustaining of a thought *because I choose to* when I might have other thoughts—need be the definition of an illusion. At any rate I will assume for the present . . . it is no illusion. My first act of free will shall be to believe in free will."[4] He further resolved that for the remainder of the year he would refrain from his usual morbid speculation "and voluntarily cultivate the feeling of moral freedom, by reading books favorable to it, as well as by action." On a new page he wrote down his new motto: "Care little for speculation/Much for the *form* of my action."

Thus in 1870 William James cultivated a belief in free will as psychiatric therapy. The previous year, under the influence of Herbert Spencer, he had been convinced that "we are Nature through and through, that we are wholly conditioned, that not a wiggle of our will happens save as the result of physical laws."[5] But now Charles Renouvier's fideism had shaken him out of his stultifying determinism and given him new hope—we might even say, new life. Actually James had first discovered Renouvier in 1868, but *Logique rationnelle* (the later title of the *Premier Essai*) did not affect him as deeply as *Psychologie rationnelle* (the revised title of *Deuxième Essai*).[6] In his "Rational Psychology" Renouvier stated his conviction that all systems of philosophy, no matter how great or famous, are expressions of the author's own temperament and character—an idea which henceforth became James's own firm conviction, and both a stimulating and consoling one for him

because it exactly fitted his own temperament. This doctrine of the
subjective basis of belief did not mean that one could simply concoct
anything he wished to believe, without regard to the objective
world. To be useful a belief must meet the test of experience, be
useful in a practical way (a foreshadowing of James's Pragmatism).
But knowledge, argued Renouvier, is always incomplete, and no
amount of statistics or logic can ever establish absolute certainty.
The result of waiting for final, irrevocable proof is, as James discovered himself, paralysis of the will. And the one thing he could
not do was sit on the fence while he saw disorder, ugliness, cruelty,
and suffering in all directions. He must be in the thick of the fight.
As he expressed it a few years later (1876) in a combination review
of Alexander Bain and Renouvier: "In every wide theoretical conclusion we must seem more or less arbitrarily to *choose* our side
. . . But if our choice is truly free, then the only possible way of
getting at that truth is by the exercise of the freedom which it
implies."[7]

Eight years later (1884) in an address to Harvard Divinity
students entitled "The Dilemma of Determinism" James produced
his own arguments for the existence of freedom to choose one's
beliefs. By this time he had found some flaws and inconsistencies
in Renouvier's arguments, but he had discovered that for himself
the moral argument outweighed all others and the arguments which
he advanced were by this time intimately personal, anticipating his
line of reasoning twelve years hence in what was to become the more
famous address, "The Will to Believe."[8]

At the outset James reminded the students of Divinity that
"evidence of external kind to decide between determinism and
indeterminism is . . . strictly impossible to find." But if they would
consider the *difference* between the two doctrines they would see
which would be more satisfactory and advantageous for them to accept. Determinism "professes that those parts of the universe already
laid down absolutely appoint and decree what the other parts
shall be. The future has no ambiguous possibilities hidden in its
womb: the part we call the present is compatible with only one
totality. Any other future complement than the one fixed from
eternity is impossible."[9] The deterministic universe is an "iron
block."

"Indeterminism, on the contrary, says that the parts have a

certain amount of loose play on one another, so that the laying down of one of them does not necessarily determine what the others shall be. It admits that possibilities may be in excess of actualities, and that things not yet revealed to our knowledge may really in themselves be ambiguous. Of two alternative futures which we conceive, both may now be really possible; and the one becomes impossible only at the very moment when the other excludes it by becoming real. Indeterminism thus denies the world to be one unbending unit of fact. It says there is a certain ultimate pluralism in it; and, so saying, it corroborates our ordinary unsophisticated view of things. To that view, actualities seem to float in a wider sea of possibilities from out of which they are chosen; and, *somewhere,* indeterminism says, such possibilities exist, and form a part of truth."

What most concerns James is *possibility.* For determinism there are no possibilities; those that "fail to get realized are . . . pure illusions: they never were possibilities at all."[10] Later in the address James switches from *possibilities* to *chance.* Determinism, of course, rules out chance completely; indeterminism accepts chance, a word from which metaphysicians shrink as if it were a pestilence. Whether this actually be a world of chance, we do not know, and can never know. All James hopes to do is show the difference between a world with chance in it and one without any possibility of chance. From the point of view of morality, the difference is enormous.

Here we come to the "dilemma" of determinism. The determinist can never find a satisfying explanation for evil in the world. "If God be good, how came he to create—or, if he did not create, how comes he to permit—the devil? The evil facts must be explained as seeming: the devil must be whitewashed, the universe must be disinfected, if neither God's goodness nor his unity and power are to remain unimpugned."[11]

What especially exercised James was that in a deterministic universe no real distinction can be made between good and bad. Things simply are, and moral distinctions are merely subjective fantasies. "Calling a thing bad means, if it mean anything at all, that the thing ought not to be, that something else ought to be in its stead. Determinism, in denying that anything else can be in its stead, virtually defines the universe as a place in which what ought to be is impossible,—in other words, an organism whose constitution is afflicted with an incurable taint, an irremediable flaw."[12] The only escape from pessimism is to abandon regret.

As always James preferred an unfinished universe, bristling with chance and possibilities; a universe in which both good and bad are real, and eternally at war. "Regarded as a stable finality, every outward good becomes a mere weariness to the flesh. It must be menaced, be occasionally lost, for its goodness to be fully felt as such. Nay, more than occasionally lost. No one knows the worth of innocence till he knows it is gone forever, and that money cannot buy it back. Not the saint, but the sinner that repenteth, is he to whom the full length and breadth, and height and depth, of life's meaning is revealed. Not the absence of vice, but vice there, and virtue holding her by the throat, seems the ideal human state. And there seems no reason to suppose it is not a permanent human state."[13]

To the question "Does not the admission of such an unguaranteed chance or freedom preclude utterly the notion of a Providence governing the world?" James replied by an analogy: "Suppose two men before a chessboard,—the one a novice, the other an expert player of the game. The expert intends to beat. But he cannot foresee exactly what any one actual move of his adversary may be. He knows, however, all the *possible* moves of the latter; and he knows in advance how to meet each of them by a move of his own which leads in the direction of victory. And the victory infallibly arrives, after no matter how devious a course, in the one predestined form of check-mate to the novice's king." In this allegory the novice stands for the finite free agent, the expert for the infinite mind. Perhaps we might think that James's analogy is itself not very optimistic, with the inevitability of defeat for the novice. But, says James, "it is immaterial . . . whether the creator leave the absolute chance-possibilities to be decided by himself, each when its proper moment arrives, or whether, on the contrary, he alienate this power from himself, and leave the decision out and out to the finite creatures such as we men are. The great point is that the possibilities are really *here*."[14]

II

In none of the works from which I have been quoting, nor in any similar ones from which I have not quoted, did William James clearly define the *will* or *volition,* though throughout the decade of the 1880s he must have been thinking about definitions as he worked on his monumental *Principles of Psychology,* which took him twelve years to complete.[15] He was thoroughly familiar with the scientific literature in German, French, and English on the chemistry and biology of the brain and on the nervous system, and with all theories on the relation of mind and body. But introspection provided his most valuable data. In a chapter on the "Automaton-Theory" he observed, "We can form no positive image of the *modus operandi* of a volition or other thought affecting the cerebral molecules."[16] He felt sure that molecular activity accompanied all thinking, but which produced the other, or why one affected the other, he did not know, and called this a metaphysical question, not a psychological one.

Consequently, in his chapter on "The Will" in his *Principles of Psychology* James avoided any consideration of the origin of a volition in motor discharges or other physiological phenomena. "In a word, volition is a psychic or moral fact pure and simple, and is absolutely completed when the stable state of the idea is there. The supervention of motion is a supernumerary phenomenon depending on executive ganglia whose function lies outside the mind." The mind becomes aware of many things without effort, through sensation and association, but volition is *attention with effort.* "*The essential achievement of the will, in short, when it is most 'voluntary,' is to ATTEND to a difficult object and hold it fast before the mind.* The so doing *is* the *fiat;* and it is a mere physiological incident that when the object is thus attended to, immediate motor consequences should ensue. A *resolve,* whose contemplated motor consequences are not to ensue until some possibly far-distant future condition shall have been fulfilled, involves all the psychic elements of a motor fiat except the word 'now'; and it is the same with many of our purely theoretic beliefs."[17]

Thus the whole drama of the will is a mental drama. And it is also a moral drama because it necessitates effort, sometimes painful effort, or unpleasant choice, demanding sacrifice of more pleasurable alternatives. Here James's own moral nature is most evident. "When a dreadful object is presented, or when life as a whole turns up its dark abysses to our view, then the worthless ones among us lose their hold on the situation altogether, and either escape from its difficulties by averting their attention, or if they cannot do that, collapse into yielding masses of plaintiveness and fear. . . . But the heroic mind does differently . . . The world . . . finds in the heroic man its worthy match and mate . . . He can *stand* this Universe . . . He can still find a zest in it, not by 'ostrich-like forgetfulness,' but by pure inward willingness to face the world with those deterrent objects there. And hereby he becomes one of the masters and the lords of life. He must be counted with henceforth; he forms a part of human destiny."[18]

One of James's strongest objections to determinism was that it refused to recognize heroes, regarding every man as a puppet of fate. In a lecture on "Great Men and Their Environment" James granted that to an infinite mind the fall of a sparrow might affect and be affected by the Milky Way, but the finite mind has no such universal knowledge, and must limit its attention. "The causes of production of great men lie in a sphere wholly inaccessible to the social philosopher."[19] But whatever their origin, individual men can and do bring about social change, which in turn affects other changes, so that a man's influence may be far-reaching in time and space.

"The mutations of society, then, from generation to generation, are in the main due directly or indirectly to the acts or the examples of individuals whose genius was so adapted to the receptivities of the moment, or whose accidental position of authority was so critical that they became ferments, initiators of movement, setters of precedent or fashion, centres of corruption, or destroyers of other persons, whose gifts, had they had free play, would have led society in another direction."[20]

This line of thinking plainly anticipated James's later "Pragmatism."[21] In 1898 in an address called "Philosophical Conceptions and Practical Results" he declared: "Beliefs, in short, are really rules for action; and the whole function of thinking is but one step in the production of habits of action . . . Thus to develop a thought's meaning we need only determine what conduct it is fitted to produce; that conduct is for us its sole significance."[22] It was this criterion of truth that many people found so upsetting.

Eight years later in *Pragmatism* James paraphrased this definition which he attributed to C. E. Peirce, and added: ". . . the tangible fact at the root of all our thought-distinctions, however subtle, is that there is no one of them so fine as to consist in anything but a possible difference of practice. To attain perfect clearness in our thoughts of an object, then, we need only consider what conceivable effects of a practical kind the object may involve—what sensations we are to expect from it, and what reactions we must prepare."[23]

If our beliefs determine our actions, and only results give meaning which can be regarded as *truth,* then the only kind of universe in which a sufficient amount of choice is possible for the human will to affect changes in environment, society, and individual lives is a pluralistic universe. Whether the universe is ultimately determined or undetermined is a metaphysical question which James says can never be answered, but on the local level each person seems to have at least sufficient freedom to enable him to make choices which assert what he thinks *ought to be,* and by such assertions both the individual and his society are changed. Every day experiences and observation confirm this belief. Now since this belief is obviously useful, we have every right to assume that it is real and not an illusion.

James's philosophical thinking culminated in *A Pluralistic Universe,* the title of the Hibbert lectures which he delivered at Oxford in 1909, just a year before his death.[24] But Pluralism was only the logical sequence of James's Pragmatism. As Ralph Barton Perry says, "Its personal roots lay in his love of variety and change; its moral roots in his unwillingness to compromise good and evil, or the individual with the universal." This love of variety and change led to James's "picturesque representation of a world which was unfenced, uncultivated, untidy, and unpredictable—a world which slipped through every ideal container, and resisted the impression of every logical mould."[25]

But this world is not haphazard, and James still believed, as he did in writing *Varieties of Religious Experience* (1902), that some kind of infinite intelligence operates at the center: "God is the natural appellation, for us Christians at least, for the supreme reality, so I will call this higher part of the universe by the name of God. We and God have business with each other; and in opening ourselves to his influence our deepest destiny is fulfilled. The universe, at those parts of it which our personal being constitutes,

takes a turn genuinely for the worse or for the better in proportion
as each one of us fulfills or evades God's demands."[26] Whether or
not this God is Himself incomplete (James seems to imply as much
in his Pluralism), He at least needs the help of human wills to
create the world that "ought to be." Man must exercise his will,
therefore, to cooperate with God.

Thus, finally, William James agreed with Emerson in his essay
on "Fate" that "freedom is necessary."[27] In fact, Emerson's paradox
on Fate is completely analogous to James's on determinism: "If you
please to plant yourself on the side of Fate, and say, Fate is all; then
we say, a part of Fate is freedom of man. Intellect annuls Fate. So
far as man thinks, he is free." William James not only agreed with
this assertion, but he also agreed for the same moral reasons: " 'Tis
the best use of Fate to teach a fatal courage . . . For if Fate is
so prevailing, man also is a part of it, and can confront fate with
fate."

NOTES

[1] For Henry James, Sr.'s own account of his revolt against his father's
Calvinism see "Immortal Life: An Autobiographical Sketch," in *The Literary Remains of Henry James,* ed. by William James (Boston, 1885), pp.
121–191. On his cultivating spontaneity, see Robert C. LeClair, *Young
Henry James* (New York, 1955), Ch. 3.

[2] See *The Letters of William James,* ed. by his son Henry James (Boston,
1920), I, 145 (hereafter referred to as *Letters*).

[3] Quoted by Ralph Barton Perry, *The Thought and Character of William James* (Boston, 1935), II, 356.

[4] *Letters,* I, 147.

[5] *Ibid.,* p. 152.

[6] Perry, I, 654, 657; Letters, I, 138.

[7] William James, *Collected Essays and Reviews* (London, 1920), pp.
33–34 (hereafter referred to as *Collected Essays*).

[8] "An Address to the Philosophical Clubs of Yale and Brown Universities," published in *New World,* June, 1896. Reprinted in *The Will to
Believe and Other Essays in Popular Philosophy* (New York, 1956).

[9] *Will to Believe* (reprint), p. 150.

[10] *Ibid.,* p. 151.

[11] *Ibid.,* p. 167.

[12] *Ibid.,* pp. 161–162.

[13] *Ibid.,* p. 169.

[14] *Ibid.,* pp. 180, 181, 183.

[15] Perry, I, 375.

[16] *The Principles of Psychology* (New York, 1950), I, 135.

[17] *Ibid.,* II, 560, 561–562.

[18] *Ibid.,* 578–579.

[19]A Lecture before the Harvard Historical Society, published in *The Atlantic Monthly*, October, 1880; reprinted in *The Will to Believe*. In the latter, see pp. 225–226; see also William James, *Selected Papers on Philosophy* (London, 1956), p. 173.

[20]*Selected Papers*, p. 174.

[21]*Pragmatism* (New York, 1907); and the "sequel," *The Meaning of Truth* (New York, 1909).

[22]Delivered at the University of California (Berkeley), *Collected Essays*, p. 410.

[23]*Selected Papers*, p. 200.

[24]As early as 1885, commenting on his father's "religious monism" (*Literary Remains*, pp. 118-119), William James said that "monism appeals to the sick soul . . . pluralism appeals to the healthy-minded," and "one must go."

[25]Perry, III, 585.

[26]Conclusion, p. 507 in the Modern Library edition (New York, n.d.); p. 399 in the Collier edition (New York, 1961).

[27]The first essay in Emerson's *Conduct of Life*. James's interest in Emerson is attested by his annotated copies of Emerson's essays, now in the Houghton Library at Harvard University.

III

Naturalistic
Determinism

❧EDGAR M. BRANCH

Freedom and Determinism in
James T. Farrell's Fiction

It is a critical commonplace that James T. Farrell's fiction reveals a thoroughgoing naturalistic determinism. Richard Mitchell and Robert Gorham Davis are among the few who disagree, and Frederick Hoffman and Charles C. Walcutt take partial exception. The usual view may be seen in Leslie Fiedler's call for the "ritual slaughter" of Farrell, a sacrifice designed to exorcise naturalism, which, he writes, with its "rigid philosophical determinism . . . finds the individual insignificant or powerless or both (and therefore not responsible morally) in the face of his environment." Malcolm Cowley also puts Farrell with the naturalists who believe in a determinism of "abstract forces" leaving men "incapable of shaping their own destinies," and Randall Stewart concurs from the Christian standpoint. This view makes Farrell's determinism central to his naturalism. It counterposes free will and determining mechanisms—personal, social, or natural. It tends to see man's destiny as an either-or alternative: either victory or helpless capitulation. Often it regards Farrell's characters as will-less puppets and usually sees them brushing feebly, with degrading results, against the crushing block of the social environment, epitomized by Chicago's "South Side."[1]

Such a view is inadequate for two reasons. It does not come to grips with the functional conception of the self informing the development of character in Farrell's fiction. Nor does it grasp the full pattern of human conduct in his fiction as a whole, a pattern that accommodates freedom. This paper will present an alternative view of Farrell's determinism and, therefore, of the ethical import of his fiction. It will suggest that his portrayal of human conduct was deeply affected by the thought of American pragmatists whom he read in the late 1920s. The first section will relate his functional conception of personality to certain key ideas he found in James, Dewey, Mead, and C. Judson Herrick, and it will then apply this conception to *Studs Lonigan* in attempting to clarify the nature of its determinism. The second section will trace the broad pattern of conduct in his fiction by relating it first to his overall subject and then to a major unifying principle in his fiction: John Dewey's ethics. For Dewey's ethical thought appears to be a shaping force throughout Farrell's fiction and not merely in *Studs Lonigan*. Perhaps we may say it works in Farrell's imagination as a myth of human liberation. In the second section my remarks will be directed mainly toward the core of Farrell's fiction, the cycles of novels centering on Studs Lonigan, Danny O'Neill, and Bernard Carr, and toward *Human Nature and Conduct,* the book that has meant more to Farrell, since he first read it in 1920, than any other of Dewey's works.

II

In June 1929 when Farrell began to write *Studs Lonigan,* he had been thinking of economic determinism in human life and the possibility of making Studs a slum dweller. But he decided that a slum setting, with its emphasis on paralyzing material poverty, would obscure an important meaning in his novel: the effect of spiritual poverty upon character. He proceeded to use his own boyhood neighborhood, one that he described in a notebook of that time as "bourgeois" and "unhappy," having "all the deadness that comfort loving middle-classness implies."[2] Furthermore he believed that individual character was cause as well as effect, for each person interacted dynamically with his culture. In the undated manuscript "The Story of Studs Lonigan" he indicated his early view: "Environment affected character, and character itself is a social product which is a result of society. In turn, character affects and changes environment." He added that Studs was not conceived as "an unwilling victim of environment."[3]

Such statements of his early views on the self and its relationships seem to be accurate. In a review published in May 1929
he discussed an article by Lawrence K. Frank "in which the
heredity-environment question is approached from the standpoint
of interaction." Farrell approvingly noted that Frank's view meant
that the organism "delimits the possible direction and expansion
which environing stimuli can produce, by its inherent capacities
. . ."[4] At this time Farrell was reading John Dewey intensively,
and his notebooks of the period refer to passages in Dewey's books.
In a notebook article of about 1930 entitled "Towards An Interpretation of Popular American Art" Farrell borrowed some of
Dewey's ideas, including his concept of civilized savages. These
persons, he wrote, "perform tasks which canalize their impulses
in rigid undynamic habits, thereby establishing a tightly-clamped
neural set-up. Impulses break loose from this narrow, drudgery-
driven confinement, and are unattached. America, being socially
chaotic, with cheap aesthetic standards, fails to provide social
meanings sufficient for free impulses . . ." The character of the
civilized savage, he continued, overstimulated by the strain and
boredom of mechanical work, helps create brothels, speakeasies,
taxi dances, cheap cabarets—all the Saturday night institutions
frequented by "the American savage in his urban jungle."[5]

By 1929 Farrell had read William James's discussion of habit
in *Principles of Psychology*. Like Dewey, James recognized the
power of inertia in habit and man's need to make habit his ally
in the creative reshaping of environment rather than his enemy
through routine. To James, habit was a fate inherent in the nerve-
cells, dooming all of us "to fight out the battle of life upon the
lines of our nurture or our early choice . . ." But choice *was*
possible, and every man spun his own fate. He insisted that no
hell is worse "than the hell we make for ourselves in this world
by habitually fashioning our characters in the wrong way."[6]
Similarly Dewey thought of habit as dynamic potentiality, an
organizing predisposition toward action. "Habit means special sen-
sitiveness or accessibility to certain classes of stimuli, standing
predilections and aversions, rather than bare recurrence of specific
acts. It means will."[7] The words of James and Dewey suggest a
view of character that went into the making of Studs and Danny
O'Neill.

In 1929 Farrell read George Herbert Mead's article "The Genesis of the Self and Social Control," in which the philosopher explored the development of the self through its social relationships. Mead echoed Dewey in believing that an individual's environment arises "through the selective power of an attention that is determined by its impulses that are seeking expression." As Whitehead had observed, each individual slices up the common life in a different manner. Each has his private environment. Mead believed that social actions, which require cooperation, are possible to the degree a person assumes the attitudes of others involved in his conduct. By taking the roles of others, by embedding their reactions in his own responses, an individual gives substance to his own self. It is this "generalized other" within experience that gives range and flexibility to the self and makes social control possible.[8]

Mead recognized the difficulty of bringing people together so that they may enter into each other's lives and thus make social control and the common endeavour possible. The difficulty, he wrote, is enormous, "for it involves not simply breaking down passive barriers such as those of distance in space and time and vernacular, but those fixed attitudes of custom and status in which our selves are imbedded. Any self is a social self, but it is restricted to the group whose roles it assumes, and it will never abandon this self until it finds itself entering into the larger society and maintaining itself there."[9]

This statement by a champion of humane rationalism and an advocate of the realistic novel has startling application to Farrell's *Studs Lonigan.* Conversely, Farrell's dramatization of spiritual poverty in Studs's personality and culture reflects one of the roads open to the self in Mead's general theory. Studs's commitment to narrow values is expressed in habitual conduct that defines his environment. So responsive is he to the chosen few, the real stuff, that paradoxically he blocks himself off from others who reach out to him, offering avenues of escape. His "generalized other" is fiercely held, but it is not general enough to prolong his life beyond twenty-nine years. His actions reveal the breakdown of control in society at large, and simultaneously they expose the rigidity and completeness of social control within the narrow world he carves out for his own. His life exhibits the isolation and consequent delusions befalling a man whose partly self-created environment is narrowly restricted.

In *Experience and Nature* Dewey stated his belief that our view of reality must make it possible for devotion, piety, mystery, beauty and love to be as real as anything else. The optimistic thrust of American pragmatism may be seen in C. Judson Herrick's *Brains of Rats and Men,* which Farrell also read in 1929. "Rats are not men" is the opening sentence of Herrick's last chapter, and its closing sentence is "Men are bigger and better than rats."[10] Rat-like behavior is instinct crystallized into habit. But human behavior, Herrick argued, is plastic and is characterized by generalization, foresight, and choice. Purpose and will can outweigh hereditary patterns and environmental pressures as causes of action. He believed that sympathy, affection, conscience, and altruistic aspiration were empirical components of human conduct. Herrick opposed the arguments of both behaviorists and mystics. He believed mind was a function of body, part of one natural world, but was not thereby explained away as a cause. When we remember that Farrell conceived Studs and Danny jointly and as opposites, it seems probable that Herrick's conception of the extremes of consciousness and action in the vertebrate realm lies behind the creation of these characters, although naturally Farrell's realism and his partial identification with each character precluded a portrait of the routine Studs as merely rat-like, and a portrait of the more aware and socialized Danny as pure creative plasticity.[11]

A brief consideration of a few incidents from *Studs Lonigan* will suggest the vital role of the foregoing ideas in shaping Farrell's conception of human character. There is little doubt that the trilogy shows character as a product of social values and institutions. Johnny O'Brien's father, who is morally corrupt, seems like the ideal father to Studs because he is a regular guy and an influential business man. Father Shannon, who is the voice of the Church of Studs, assails godless universities, modern literature, and secular thought. He becomes the model for bigotry and the justification for violence in Studs and his friends.

We notice the poverty of alternatives Studs's society offers him. On the beach with Catherine just before his heart attack in Lake Michigan, he comes about as close as he can to self-recognition. He cannot understand the causes of his plight, but he sees some facts clearly. Momentarily he is humble in his accurate self-appraisal. He feels weak and powerless before his problems, and completely alone. His real self is padlocked within. Seeing the sky and clouds above, he "thought of what a big place the world was after all, and he was sort of lost in it. He felt that he had always been like this" (JD, 335).* Having belittled Catherine in his thoughts, "he suddenly asked himself who the hell he was, wanting so damn much, and thinking she wasn't enough for him" (JD, 335). But Studs has not learned to base his habits upon his individual perceptions and innermost feelings. He usually acts conventionally, and in imagination his responses become increasingly atrophied and trite. The self-revelation in this scene momentarily breaks through the crust of his stereotyped notions of himself, only to fizzle out in his pitiful wish that "he were a six-foot handsome bastard, built like a full-back, attracting the attention of the crowd of bathers" (JD, 335). What might in another have been the prelude to contrition and change, in Studs is channeled away from action into one of the banal images of greatness accepted in his culture. The impulse toward truth and reform is dissipated in social cliché—the puny vestige of a once rather vigorous imagination in the boy.

Similarly *Studs Lonigan* is concerned with the creation of social effects and institutions through character. Studs and his friends patronize poolrooms, brothels, and dance halls. Their sadistic jokes, the rapes and beatings, the instigation of race-riots are all to the point here. The book constantly returns to the social disorganization or stagnation that is rooted in human will. We see the process in the details of action. Jewboy Schwartz is maimed by Studs's team. The restaurant owner Gus fires Christy, his radical waiter, after complaints from his customers. Because he is kidded about Lucy, Studs leaves his friends from Indiana Avenue to join the tough lads from Fifty-eighth and Prairie. He is accepted, life opens up. He brings his natural leadership with him, and the gang grows before our eyes.

---

*Quotations from *Studs Lonigan: A Trilogy* are from the Modern Library edition and will be documented in the text. The symbols YL, YMSL, and JD represent *Young Lonigan, The Young Manhood of Studs Lonigan,* and *Judgment Day.*

Studs does not lack will, for a major point of the trilogy is his constant and painful hacking at his humanity. As a boy Studs is often hopeful, imaginative, aware of his feelings, sensitive to criticism. His standards are naive and unenlightened, yet he is sharply aware of the difference between right and wrong. Morally he is often at odds with himself; he knows aspiration and guilt. Even toward the end his life holds potentiality for good as well as for evil. His understanding grows in some respects. He is never really a tough guy, and the slob never loses his conscience. Fundamental to Studs's degradations and self-destruction is an idealism and a romantic flair. He wills to be tough precisely because the unpredictable tender feelings and need for love are strong within him and because toughness, he has learned, can be controlled and can get results. Studs's tough-guy attitude is his bid for self-fulfillment. His obstinate pursuit of toughness, despite his inner feelings and even—ludicrously—as a twenty-nine–year–old weakling and runt in *Judgment Day,* shows the strength of his commitment. Studs's misdirected will, in short, is always evident.

Knowing Lucy still likes him and facing her loss unless he trusts his devotion, Studs nevertheless tries "to make himself feel good by telling himself how tough he was" (YL, 170). It does not work. He still loves Lucy but he sticks to his ideal of toughness. He is proud. "After all he was STUDS LONIGAN" (YL, 169). Another boy, Huck Finn, tried to make himself feel good by doing the conventional and inhuman thing. It did not work for him either. But he proceeded to fool the Negro-hunters and later he tore up the letter to Miss Watson. Thus in some of his loyalties and actions, Studs begins as a kind of truncated Huck, but he ends as his opposite. Each is sensitive to the ideal of human communion, but Studs learns not to will it. Instead he wills his own isolated hell. He thinks he is "the real stuff" (YMSL, 411), but he denies his best impulses. Huck affirms his in action, but without full comprehension. He wills the godlike within, although in typical humility he thinks it is the devil. The difference is fundamentally a difference in character, and each boy's character may be regarded as a social product and a human force affecting society. Studs's society is more restricted and congealed than Huck's wide world. The results of man's evil are more easily compounded in it. Yet its corruptions are qualitatively no greater and it too provides sources of spiritual strength and images of courage and love. Studs, for example, senses the integrity of Connolly, the Bug Club speaker from the University of Chicago. But his darkened will knows only how to vigorously condemn the University and all learning. One glorious afternoon Studs sits in the Washington Park tree with Lucy, "a prayer sprung into flesh" (YL, 115). But in the dark he steers Elizabeth Burns, the diseased "fourteen-year-old bitch" (YMSL, 67), to a spot on the ground "near the tree where he and Lucy had been" (YMSL, 81). Studs constantly wills his own victimization.

Studs's relation to experience is symbolized well in *Judgment Day* when he offers a pint of blood during his initiation into the Order of Christopher. As part of a rigged initiation stunt, Judge Gorman, the master of ceremonies, asks that a volunteer give his blood in symbolic proof of the serious intention of all initiates to assume their responsibilities within the Order. He insists the act "must be absolutely voluntary" (JD, 151). Studs, an easy mark, immediately imagines himself as "one made to stand out and make others cheer for him" (JD, 150). Although he cannot afford the blood, he tries to believe guts will carry him through his supreme opportunity "to show the real stuff in him" (JD, 151). Hesitating, afraid, he is impelled to act when another volunteers. "Yellow? Studs Lonigan yellow? Without will or thought, he shot up his right hand, and said, with a rush of breath: 'I will!' " (JD, 151). He edges his way to the speaker's stand, his lips "clamped tight with determination" (JD, 153). The decisive motivation is the horror at his self-accusation of "yellow" which overrides his fear of death, just as his willed toughness is capable of obliterating other emotions. The "absolutely voluntary" act *is* voluntary for Studs. In his poor physical condition he believes his offer of blood might lead to death. He sees the alternatives: possible death or the inner uncleanliness of knowing himself yellow. So thoroughly has he adopted the tough-guy ideal that he acts as though "without will or thought" in his rush to volunteer. Thus the determining factor is his decision, his choice between two difficult alternatives. In this respect Studs is not determined in a crude or simple way. Yet he acts from a background of shallowness and darkness, and he does not suspect he is the victim of a hoax. Ignorant and shoddily motivated, he emerges from his past to rush into the future a sucker—and a still frustrated hero of lost opportunity.

Studs is a dupe, but a vigorously cooperative one: a dupe of his time and place, and equally of his sensitivity and idealism. For his environment "takes" on him all too well because of his sensitivity and his desire for recognition. Lucy's feeling for him, Helen Shires's friendship, Davey Cohen's involvement with him, and Andy LeGare's testimony that "Stutz Lonigan is the bes whitest guy of the older guy who hang around that pool roome den of iniquieties" (YMSL, 184) all affirm his innate worth. Studs comes close to the average person who fails to realize his potential and descends to disaster. His ideal stature is best seen in his vision of felicity with Lucy, a quickly destroyed possibility but one destroyed through his own actions. His emotions and his mind atrophy as he progressively wills his destruction, from ignorance within and around him, until, in *Judgment Day*, regretful, somewhat aware, and more flexible than usual in his human relations, he finds it is too late.

We know that *Studs Lonigan* did not arise primarily from Farrell's desire to illustrate a sociological thesis or a philosophic position. It arose from very personal needs and powerful emotions coupled with a keen interest in the mystery of human character. But the writing of *Studs Lonigan* and of later works was directly affected by Farrell's creative use of ideas encountered in his reading of the late 1920s. Among these were ideas expressed by leading American pragmatists, especially concepts of habit, will, and the interaction of the individual and his culture. These concepts helped Farrell to clarify his thoughts about human behavior and corroborated what he already had grasped emotionally. Thus they strengthened his confidence in himself as an interpreter of his past, and they supported his tension-laden compulsion to explore his experience more deeply by recreating it in fiction. They helped him to give fictional shape to the "tendencies"—a favorite term of Dewey's—he had felt and seen at work in long years of deeply absorbed experience. Above all else, perhaps, they entered into his characterizations by providing him with a concept of the functional relationship of self to society. This is a union in which the self is both passive and active partner. The self is conceived as subject to events but also as a power, whether for good or ill, in its own right. It is a candidate for a genuine but limited freedom, and ironically its capacity for free action may be expressed in a bondage that is partly self-imposed.

III

The pattern of human conduct that emerges from Farrell's fiction as a whole allows for both freedom and bondage within society, and it reveals a clear progression from bondage through growing awareness to responsible freedom. This pattern should be seen in the context of Farrell's subject and themes.

His fiction explores the ethical significance of time, the process of human change defined by the interaction between individual and society. His people are drawn from four generations and their actions span half a century. Most of them are part of an urban America that is moving away from plebeian crudity toward a degree of cultural sophistication. As Farrell wrote to Van Wyck Brooks, his concern is with "the American way of life," a subject that for him presupposes both the social making of character and the origin of social consequences within character.[12] His subject thus becomes the unity of personal and national American growth within the "social universe" of his experience.[13] His character Bernard Carr strikes the important keynote in wondering how he, once an ordinary boy in Chicago, had found his way to being an important New York writer. Similarly Studs Lonigan wonders what went wrong with his life. Whether Farrell's characters are defeated or fulfilled, and whether change in their lives approaches stagnancy or abrupt rebellion, Farrell seeks detailed answers to the questions "What happened?" and "How did it happen?" As he brings his characters forward in time, he identifies the seeds that have flowered as qualities of heart and mind while simultaneously he traces further consequences of their expanding or constricting values—the never-ending process of social interaction. Within the framework of a naturalism that assumes final oblivion for all men, he writes about education for life and education for death. He explores growth, self-discovery, creativity—and their frustration. These are his themes, and the business of his fiction is to trace the human destinies of his scores of characters in their intricate social web.

The ethical thrust of Farrell's subject appears clearly in the dramatic pattern formed by the three cycles of novels about Studs, Danny, and Bernard. The eleven novels of these series are the heart of a single fable tracing the rise of a type of twentieth-century American male—urban, Irish-Catholic, aspiring—from a condition of ignorance and human waste to a state of growing independence and useful self-fulfillment. It is a fable of emergence, of growth into liberation and responsibility, in which Studs represents the life Danny rejects, and Bernard the life Danny chooses. The emergent destiny is a hopeful one affirming love and the creative power of mind and will. The outcome presupposes free will not as an endowment, nor as a transcendental attribute of soul isolated from worldly desire, but as an achievement won through the control of environment and of self made possible by knowledge. This central fable illustrates Danny O'Neill's statement in *Boarding House Blues*: "A life is blown by a wind called destiny, and that wind is controlled by the mind as much as by circumstances."[14]

Danny's words are a kind of shorthand for John Dewey's philosophy of freedom, which Farrell first defended in print in 1930.[15] Danny's "wind called destiny," or the events making up a life, implies Dewey's concept of reality as "a moving affair,"* a flowing experience bringing genuine contingency in an open world where "accounts are still in process of making" (310). The circumstances that Danny believes partially control man's destiny are fully recognized by Dewey, whose doctrine of "the continuity of mind with nature" (186) places man firmly within his environment. "We live mentally as physically," writes Dewey, "only *in* and *because* of our environment" (327). "There are in truth," he says, "forces in man as well as without him" (10). Native tendencies, habits, customs, institutions, and all that gives organization to experience, are confining elements. And experience, he writes, constantly awakens "a sense of our dependence upon forces that go their way without our wish and plan" (289).

Where, then, for Dewey, lies the possibility of freedom? Danny's mention of mind, which partially controls the wind of destiny, suggests Dewey's answer. Dewey recognizes that "there is

---

Human Nature and Conduct (New York, 1922), p. 239. Hereafter quotations from this book are documented parenthetically in the text.

no . . . objective freedom without organization" (306); all life must operate through mechanisms, whether they are psychological, social, or natural. The hopeful fact is that habits and institutions are confining because, more fundamentally, they are liberating agencies of intelligence to effect men's will. As problems change, then, forms and organizations may be altered by the "unremitting application" (306) of knowledge to conditions. For Dewey, "intelligence is the key to freedom in act" (304). He recognizes genuine choice but makes intelligent deliberation the essential factor in freedom, for by intelligent deliberation we may successfully "use one 'necessity' to alter another" (312) and thus make creative, directed change possible. His ethics avoids both the transcendental position of "severing . . . [morals and freedom] from actual facts and forces" and the deterministic position "that natural laws are themselves moral laws, so that it remains, after noting them, only to conform to them" (296).

Some will say, Dewey notes, that if "deliberation determines choice and deliberation is determined by character and conditions," then there is no freedom. Dewey answers: "This is like saying that because a flower comes from root and stem it cannot bear fruit. The question is not what are the antecedents of deliberation and choice, but what are their consequences. What do . . . [deliberation and choice] do that is distinctive? The answer is that they give us all the control of future possibilities which is open to us. And this control is the crux of our freedom. Without it, we are pushed from behind. With it we walk in the light" (311). In Farrell's fiction Studs Lonigan is pushed from behind by his routine habits—outmoded, rigid clichés of thought and action ultimately inadequate to his survival. His story gives us the birth and anatomy of the enslaved man. Danny O'Neill begins to walk in the light, for he acquires the habit of acquiring knowledge, a tool for shaping his future. His story relates the long gestation and the birth of the free man who, if he cannot forget his past, plans to use it creatively. Bernard Carr learns that the successful control of his future as a free man does indeed require constant deliberation and choice, ultimately expressed as an intelligent loyalty to the truth of experience. His story becomes the early history of the responsible man who gives positive meaning to freedom through his art and his human relationships.

Farrell's doctrine that character functions both as social product and as social cause reflects Dewey's answer to his own question: How can individuals, who are caught up within social groups, nevertheless "remake and redirect" (60) old customs? In Studs Lonigan Farrell creates a sense of inevitability by stressing character as social product, the result of "social processes of evil," to use his phrase for an important effect of Dreiser's.[16] As Richard Mitchell has shown, Studs is Dewey's "creature of habit" (125) with the "pigeon-hole" (39) mind incapable of genuine thinking. Also he fits Dewey's concept of the savage within civilization who achieves the illusion of freedom through the blind, violent discharge of impulse, and who compensates through fantasy for his "submerged and humiliated" (158) self. He is a stunted caricature of Dewey's ideal child, in whom "growth is normal not an anomaly, activity [is] a delight not a task, and . . . habit-forming is an expansion of power not its shrinkage" (99). We never doubt that Studs the child is father to the man.

Likewise Dewey's analysis of moral and social retrogression is a guidebook to landmarks of Studs's culture: "adult custom . . . strengthening tendencies toward conformity" (97–98); the quest for certainty "born of fear of the new and of attachment to possessions" (237); education that "becomes the art of taking advantage of the helplessness of the young" (64); church and families that try to solve problems of "contemporary fluidity" (129) by "exhortations to restore old habits in their former rigidity" (130). Yet, as has been elaborated elsewhere,[17] the trilogy does not let us forget the larger world of intelligence and humane values. Also, as we have seen above, it portrays character as social cause. Studs actively shapes his restrictive environment, and he does not entirely lack will in Dewey's sense of the word as pro-jective disposition that organizes action. The seeming inevitability of his death is convincing, but we know it might have been other-wise. Studs Lonigan is not a work of monolithic determinism.

Danny O'Neill follows the course Dewey marks out for break-ing "the vicious circle" (127) of self-perpetuating customs. His dif-ficult position as a son in two families is fortunate insofar as it sets up "conflicting patterns" that, Dewey shows, "release impulse for new adventures" (128). His intense striving for recognition, first through sports, then learning, and then writing, promotes the kind of creativity Dewey attributes to sublimation. Thus he displays the élan that Dewey defines as "the peering, the search, the inquiry . . . the movement into the unknown" (180), the spirit that is the "beginning of individuality in mind" when it "asserts itself deliberately against an existing custom . . ." (87–88). Quite unlike Studs, he often can utilize impulse to "grasp and realize genuine opportunity" (234). Relatively early in life he begins to form the habit of rationality, which, Dewey says, "sets up an attitude of criticism . . . and makes men sensitive to the brutalities and extravagancies of customs" (77–78). His university education is a final stage in what Dewey calls "breaking down old rigidities of habit and preparing the way for acts that re-create an environment" (57). Danny's flexibility becomes the measure of his freedom. It contrasts with the rigidity of Al and Peg O'Flaherty, among others.

Bernard Carr fits Dewey's portrayal of the dynamic self "still [in the] making through action" (139) and seeking a more inclusive identity. From first to last, Bernard is "chasing understanding" of himself and of society, so that he may increasingly "assert his freedom from circumstance."[18] Eventually he defines himself vis-à-vis his boyhood past, the economic order, his lovers and wife, and especially the American Communist Party. His art, which is deeply concerned with self-understanding, becomes a means of integration. He learns that to write truthfully he must always remain sensitive to the flux of experience—to *his* feelings and thoughts—and must discount all systems claiming perfection and finality; "for other and yet other waters are ever flowing on."[19] As Dewey puts it, "principles treated as fixed rules . . . take men away from experience" (238), a cardinal sin. Bernard's final moral insight leads him to seek the attainable good in the present and not to locate it in a fantasy of the past or future, as Studs does, or in a Utopia of this world, as the Communists do, or in a heaven of the next, as the Catholic Church does. Dewey asserts that his is "a gospel of present growth" (284), and "In morals . . . the good is now or never" (289–290). Also he insists that reason, like virtue, is a function of "fullness of meaning of the present" (274). Memory, observation, foresight—the tools of reason—are indispensable, but, Dewey writes, "they are indispensable *to* a present liberation, an enriching growth of action" (265). This is Bernard's wisdom.

"A present liberation, an enriching growth of action": these words summarize Dewey's faith. If by freedom Dewey means enriching growth, then growth entails "variability, initiative, innovation, departure from routine, experimentation," the human traits, he says, "that are precious to us under the name of freedom" (310). In Farrell's fiction men's rigid habits, their customs and institutions, and the physical deterioration of their bodies ending in death are limits on freedom. Farrell's recognition of these limits constitutes the element of necessity or determinism in his view of man. But his fiction also shows that restrictions may stimulate, that will and reason may revolutionize a life. With Dewey's philosophy it asserts the plasticity of the self and the self's definition through interaction with the world. On this view nothing man is or does is apart from the changing continuities of existence, yet liberation from old ties is possible. Farrell's naturalism, quite simply, is the belief that all events are part of a single moving process, or, as he puts it, it is the belief in the natural origin of all events, including those human powers that permit men to shape their future for good or for ill. His fiction as a whole supports his statement: "I am not a monistic determinist."[20]

Why has the ethical import of Farrell's writing been so frequently misinterpreted? It appears that critics at times have been prisoners of a mechanistic conception of necessity—what may be termed the bulldozer view of determinism. Secondly, the image of freedom in his fiction lacks a traditional aura. It is neither a transcendental endowment nor an unmotivated, purely inner condition. Then, too, *Studs Lonigan,* a story of disintegration, is more powerful than the Bernard Carr books, and Farrell's characters who are capable of freedom, although major figures, are outnumbered by those in bondage. Finally, Farrell confronts the problem of freedom with overwhelming integrity in his best work: he recognizes the free act in its full context of impediments and contraries, including the rigid habits, the festering ignorance, and the savage, self-destructive outbursts that also are part of the life process.

NOTES

[1]See Richard Mitchell, "*Studs Lonigan*: Research in Morality," *Centennial Review,* VI (1962), 202-214; Robert Gorham Davis, "New Chapter in the Farrell Story," *New York Times Book Review,* May 12, 1963, pp. 1,

43; Frederick J. Hoffman, *The Modern Novel in America: 1900–1950* (Chicago, 1951), pp. 142–146; Charles C. Walcutt, *American Literary Naturalism, A Divided Stream* (Minneapolis, 1956), pp. 240–257; Leslie Fiedler, "Naturalism and Ritual Slaughter," *New Leader,* XXXI (Dec. 18, 1948), 10; Malcolm Cowley, "'Not Men': A Natural History of American Naturalism," *KR,* IX (1947), 414–435; Randall Stewart, *American Literature and Christian Doctrine* (Baton Rouge, 1958), pp. 107, 113, 120.

2Untitled Notebook, probably 1929 and 1930, p. 25. University of Pennsylvania Library. Copyright © 1964, James T. Farrell.

3University of Pennsylvania Library. Copyright © 1964, James T. Farrell. Compare Farrell's statement in 1940: "I hold a functional conception of character, viewing it as a social product embodying the reciprocal play of local influences on the individual, and of the individual on society. I am concerned with the concrete processes whereby society, through the instrumentality of social institutions, forms and molds characters, giving to the individual the very content of his consciousness." *New Republic,* CIII (Oct. 28, 1940), 596.

4"Ingredients of the 'Personality,'" *Chicago Evening Post Literary Review,* May 31, 1929, p. 7. This is a review of *Personality and the Social Group,* edited by E. W. Burgess.

5Untitled Notebook, probably 1929 and 1930, p. 45. University of Pennsylvania Library. Copyright © 1964, James T. Farrell. The background from which Farrell writes is indicated by this passage of Dewey's on the savage personality and the roles of impulse and habit in conduct: "Thus enslavement to custom and license of impulse exist side by side. Strict conformity and unrestrained wildness intensify each other. This picture of life shows us in an exaggerated form the psychology current in civilized life whenever customs harden and hold individuals enmeshed. Within civilization, the savage still exists. He is known in his degree by oscillation between loose indulgence and stiff habit.

"Impulse in short brings with itself the possibility but not the assurance of a steady reorganization of habits to meet new elements in new situations. The moral problem in child and adult alike as regards impulse and instinct is to utilize them for formation of new habits, or what is the same thing, the modification of an old habit so that it may be adequately serviceable under novel conditions. The place of impulse in conduct as a pivot of readjustment, re-organization, in habits may be defined as follows: On one side it is marked off from the territory of arrested and encrusted habits. On the other side, it is demarcated from the region in which impulse is a law unto itself. . . . Impulse is a source, an indispensable source, of liberation; but only as it is employed in giving habits pertinence and freshness does it liberate power." *Human Nature and Conduct* (New York, 1922), pp. 104–105.

6William James, *Principles of Psychology* (New York, 1923), I, 121, 127.

7John Dewey, *Human Nature and Conduct* (New York, 1922), p. 42.

8George H. Mead, "The Genesis of the Self and Social Control," *International Journal of Ethics,* XXXV (April, 1925), 256, 268.

9*Ibid.,* p. 276.

10C. Judson Herrick, *Brains of Rats and Men* (Chicago, 1926), pp. 347, 365.

[11]Herrick concludes: "In so far as I do thus consciously participate in the shaping of daily conduct in the light of its future effects, I am also a partner in the business of shaping my own inner nature; I am engaged in character-building as a purposeful enterprise. My part in this process is real. I can and do control, to some extent, my own destiny in ways that rats do not and cannot, for I have powers of imagination, of ratiocination, of prevision, of idealization, and of volition which they lack." *Brains of Rats and Men*, pp. 359–360.

Herrick's viewpoint is not rigorously thought out as is Dewey's and Mead's, but like theirs it combines philosophic naturalism and humanism to explain human character and action. His idealism is emotionally expressed, and he tends to uncritically polarize habitual and non-habitual actions. Nor does he present thinking as problem-solving, as Dewey does, or dissect intricate social interaction, as Mead does: analyses going a long way to help explain crucial differences between Danny and Studs. Yet his ideas remain relevant to Farrell's naturalism. In an early letter to the Editor of *The Saturday Review of Literature* Farrell linked Dewey and Herrick as naturalists who believe mind and reflective thought to be "natural functions of the human being who exists in a natural situation." See "John Dewey's Philosophy," *SRL*, VI (July 12, 1930), 1194.

[12]Letter dated March 24, 1941. University of Pennsylvania Library. Copyright © 1964, James T. Farrell.

[13]Letter to Philip M. Hicks, September 28, 1948. University of Pennsylvania Library. Copyright © 1964, James T. Farrell.

[14]New York, 1961, p. 211.

[15]Farrell, "John Dewey's Philosophy," *op. cit.* This letter responded to Lewis Mumford's "A Modern Synthesis," *SRL, VI* (April 12, 1930), 920–921. Farrell wrote: "Dr. Dewey's naturalism embraces the concept of existence from which mind emerges. And the emergence of mind, of the power of reflective thought, delimits man's path to freedom and control from the perils of the universe. . . . In 'How We Think,' Dr. Dewey has specifically stated that freedom was to be achieved by thought; is this a craven posture? In 'Experience and Nature,' he makes an explicit confession of faith. . . . In 'The Quest for Certainty' . . . Dr. Dewey explicitly criticizes the determinists and mechanists, who shoved nature outside of an interacting natural situation, making it a predetermined set of relationships. Such an attitude he set down as the reverse of the classic which makes of rational thought a predetermined set of relationships; and he reads both attitudes aside."

In addition to *Human Nature and Conduct* (1922) and Dewey's works mentioned above, Farrell read at least these books by Dewey in 1929 and 1930: *The School and Society*, Rev. Ed. (1915), *Reconstruction in Philosophy* (1920), *The Public and Its Problems* (1927), and *Individualism, Old and New* (1930). Statement by Farrell to the author, March 15, 1957.

[16]*The League of Frightened Philistines* (New York, 1945), p. 19.

[17]See Edgar M. Branch, *"Studs Lonigan: Symbolism and Theme," CE,* XXIII (1961), 191–196; "Destiny, Culture, and Technique: *Studs Lonigan," UKCR*, XXIX (1962), 103–113.

[18]The first quotation is from *Yet Other Waters* (New York, 1952), p. 411, and the second is from *Bernard Clare* (New York, 1946), p. 3.

[19]Letter from Farrell to James Henle, October 31, 1941. University

of Pennsylvania Library. Copyright © 1964, James T. Farrell. Farrell is quoting Heraclitus to explain his choice of title for the third volume of the Bernard Carr trilogy.

[20]*Reflections at Fifty and Other Essays* (New York, 1954), p. 148.

◆JOHN LYDENBERG

Dos Passos's *U.S.A.*:
The Words of the Hollow Men

BECAUSE James Baldwin, like Tocqueville a decade or more ago, has now become so fashionable that one cannot decently take a text from him, I shall start with Yevgeny Yevtushenko, in the hope that he has not quite yet reached that point. In one of his poems appear the simple lines: "Let us give back to words/Their original meanings." My other non-Dos Passos text is so classic that it cannot be over-fashionable. In *A Farewell to Arms*, Gino says, "What has been done this summer cannot have been done in vain." And, as you all know, Hemingway has Frederic Henry reply: "I did not say anything. I was always embarrassed by the words sacred, glorious, and sacrifice and the expression in vain. . . . Abstract words such as glory, honor, courage, or hallow were obscene."

These quotations suggest the concern of writers with abstract words representing the ideals and values of their society. Both Yevtushenko and Hemingway say that these words have lost their glory, their true meaning. But they take diametrically opposed attitudes toward the role the words will play in their writings. Representing the party of Hope, Yevtushenko is the social and political idealist, the reformer, the artist who sees his art as a weapon in man's unceasing struggle for a better world. Representing the party of Despair, Hemingway abjures political concerns, makes his separate peace, and develops an art unconcerned with social ideals. Thus they symbolize two extremes: writers at

97

one pole—Yevtushenko's—will utilize the words, will insist on doing so; writers at the other—Hemingway's—will dispense with them altogether, or try to do so, as did Hemingway in most of his early fiction.

Dos Passos falls between the extremes, but instead of presenting us with a golden mean he gives something more like an unstable compound of the two. Hemingway abandons the words because he can see no relation between them and the realities, and creates a world stripped of the values represented by the words. By contrast, reformers—who are equally insistent on the disparity between the ideals and the realities—are unwilling to reject the words and strive, like Yevtushenko, to give back to them their original meanings. Dos Passos can neither abandon nor revivify the words. Like Hemingway he feels that they have been made obscene and he can find no way in his art to redeem them. Yet like any reformer he puts them at the center of his work.

Critics have often held that the protagonist of *U.S.A.* is society. I could almost maintain that it is, instead, "the words." Dos Passos seems obsessed by them: he cares about them passionately and cannot abandon them, but at the same time he is made sick at heart—nay at stomach—by the way they have been spoiled. So he concerns himself with problems of social values, ever returning to the words, "as a dog to his vomit" (to use the inelegant but expressive Biblical phrase). *U.S.A.* tastes sour because the words are tainted and indigestible, but neither here nor in his other fiction can Dos Passos spew them forth once and for all as could the Hemingways of our literature.

In two well-known passages, Dos Passos makes explicit his feeling about the words. These—the most eloquent and deeply felt parts of *U.S.A.*— are the Camera Eyes focused on the execution of Sacco and Vanzetti. In the first, immediately preceding the Mary French section on the last desperate days before the executions, he asks:

> how make them feel who are your oppressors America
> rebuild the ruined words worn slimy in the mouths of lawyers district-attorneys collegepresidents judges   without the old words the immigrants haters of oppression brought to Plymouth how can you know who are your betrayers America . . . ? (*Big Money*, 437)

In the second, after the execution, he says:

we the beaten crowd together . . . sit hunched with bowed heads on
benches and hear the old words of the haters of oppression   made new in
sweat and agony tonight
   our work is over   the scribbled phrases   the nights typing releases
the smell of the printshop the sharp reek of newprinted leaflets   the rush
for Western Union stringing words into wires the search for stinging words
to make you feel who are your oppressors America
   America our nation has been beaten by strangers who have turned our
language inside out who have taken the clean words our fathers spoke and
made them slimy and foul (462)*

Just as Dos Passos makes the Sacco-Vanzetti affair symbolic
of his vision of the state of the nation, so, in talking about the
"old words," "the clean words our fathers spoke," and "the old
American speech," he is alluding to his ideals, to the American
dream, and in describing the words now as "ruined," "slimy and
foul," and "turned . . . inside out," he is expressing his sense of
the betrayal of the dream.

"Mostly U.S.A. is the speech of the people," says Dos Passos
to conclude the prose poem he added as preface to the trilogy.
Maybe. But *U.S.A.*, the novel, in no way carries out that Sandburg-
like suggestion of faith in the people and delight in their talk. It
contains none of the salty talk, the boastful talk, the folksy talk,
the "wise" talk that is the staple of much "realistic" American
fiction. Actually, we discover, on re-examination of these novels,
that dialogue plays a smaller role than we might have thought
it did. What little talk there is is either purely functional, merely
a way of getting on with the narrative: "Shall we go to bed?"
"Where can I get a drink?" "God I feel lousy this morning."
Or it is banal and stereotyped. Whenever his characters express
anything resembling ideas they talk only in tired slogans; the
words have been drained of meaning, and the characters mouth-
ing them are empty puppets.

Here is one example. I would give many more, had I time,
for the real effect is gained only through the continuous repeti-
tion of the vaporous phrases. This is from *1919*, the novel written during the time Dos Passos was presumably most favorably
inclined toward Marxism and the Communists. One might have
expected that here if anywhere the words of a communist, Don

*Page references documenting the quotations from *U.S.A.* are to the
Modern Library edition (1937); those for *First Encounter* (originally published as *One Man's Initiation*) are to the New York, 1945, edition.

Stevens in this instance, would carry some conviction. Instead Dos Passos makes them sound mechanical, false, flat, like counterfeit coins. The effect is heightened here, as in many other places, by giving us the words in indirect dialog.

He said that there wasn't a chinaman's chance that the U.S. would keep out of the war; the Germans were winning, the working class all over Europe was on the edge of revolt, the revolution in Russia was the beginning of the worldwide social revolution and the bankers knew it and Wilson knew it; the only question was whether the industrial workers in the east and the farmers and casual laborers in the middle west and west would stand for war. The entire press was bought and muzzled. The Morgans had to fight or go bankrupt. "It's the greatest conspiracy in history." (131)

This is the way the words sound in passage after passage. The ruined words dribble from the mouths of Dos Passos' hollow men. Within is nothing but clichés, phrases having no meaning for the speaker and conveying none to the listener. *This* is the speech of the people in Dos Passos's *U.S.A.*, and it does much to establish the tone of the whole trilogy.

But if the words are often empty and meaningless, they often too have a very real meaning, vicious and perverted. The old words of the American dream have been "turned . . . inside out"; now they are the lies by which the new Americans live. The theme of the transformation of the clean words into lies had been baldly stated in Dos Passos's first novel, *One Man's Initiation*. Early in the book, Martin Howe dreams romantically of his mission as the ocean steamer carries him "over there": "And very faintly, like music heard across the water in the evening, blurred into strange harmonies, his old watchwords echo a little in his mind. Like the red flame of the sunset setting fire to opal sea and sky, the old exaltation, the old flame that would consume to ashes all the lies in the world, the trumpet-blast under which the walls of Jericho would fall down, stirs and broods in the womb of his grey lassitude" (14). Then as Martin is first going up to the front, he comes to adopt a new conception in which the lies are all-inclusive, his "old watchwords" now no different from the rest of the world's lies. A stranger appears and explains it to him: "Think, man, think of all the oceans of lies through all the ages that must have been necessary to make this possible! Think of this new particular vintage of lies that has been so industriously pumped out of the press and the pulpit. . . . [The] lies are like a sticky juice over-spreading the world, a living, growing flypaper to catch and gum the wings of every human soul" (30). Finally, Martin talks in much the same way himself: " 'What terrifies me . . . is their power to enslave our minds. . . . America, as you know, is ruled by the press. . . . People seem to so love to be fooled. . . . We are slaves of bought intellect, willing slaves' " (144). And a French anarchist takes up the theme and makes the moral explicit: " 'Oh, but we are all such dupes. . . . First we must fight the lies. It is the lies that choke us' " (156).

In *U.S.A.*, Dos Passos does not *tell* us about the lies, he makes us feel them. The Newsreels are his most obvious device for showing us the "sticky juice" of lies in which Americans are caught. The opening lines of *The 42nd Parallel* are: "It was that emancipated race/That was chargin up the hill;/Up to where them insurrectos/Was afightin fit to kill." The hill is not San Juan but a hill in the Philippines. And that first Newsreel ends with Senator Beveridge's Lucid bluster: "The twentieth century will be American. American thought will dominate it. American progress will give it color and direction. American deeds will make it illustrious. . . . The regeneration of the world, physical as well as moral, has begun, and revolutions never move backwards" (5).

One recognizable pattern keeps recurring in the shifting kaleidoscope of the Newsreels: that is—the official lies disguised as popular truths. We see—and hear—the rhetoric of the American Way drummed into the heads of the American public, by advertisements, newspaper headlines, newspaper stories, politicians' statements, businessmen's statements. In contrast to these standardized verbalizations about happy, prosperous, good America, the Newsreels give continual flashes of Dos Passos's "real" America—of fads and follies, hardships and horrors. More striking even than the contrasts within these collages are those between the shimmering surface of the Newsreels and the sardonic realities of the Portraits, and above all the dreary lives of his fictional characters.

The narratives of these lives take up the greater part of the book, of course, and our reaction to it depends to a great extent on our evaluation of the characters. My suggestion is that it is by their use of "the words" that we judge them. And here, *mirabile dictu*, we come at last to the theme of "determinism."

That *U.S.A.* is strongly naturalistic and deterministic is obvious to all. Readers who judge it a major work of fiction do so in part because of its success in portraying characters as helpless individuals caught in a world they have not made and can not control. Less admiring critics are apt to consider its weakness to be the weakness of the characters, sometimes even implying that Dos Passos's failure to create free, responsible heroes was a failure of execution. Whatever their assessment of the novel, all agree that *U.S.A.* is starkly deterministic. None of its characters has free will, none determines his fate, all move like automatons.

The chief way in which Dos Passos makes us feel that his characters—or non-characters—are determined is by showing their choices as non-choices. In *U.S.A.* Dos Passos's people do not make decisions. Or, if you insist that human beings all make decisions, choose one road over another, I will say instead that he presents his characters to us so that we do not feel their choices to be decisions. They simply are doing so and so, and continue thus until they find themselves, or we find them, doing something else.

Here are two examples. The first, a long one, includes two decisions, one a reversal of the other. Note here—for future reference—what the protagonist, Richard Ellsworth Savage, does with the words, and note also how the indirect dialogue accentuates the feeling of cliché and slogan. Dick is "deciding" what he should do about the war and about his college education.

In the Easter vacation, after the Armed Ship Bill had passed Dick had a long talk with Mr. Cooper who wanted to get him a job in Washington, because he said a boy of his talent oughtn't to endanger his career by joining the army and already there was talk of conscription. Dick blushed becomingly and said he felt it would be against his conscience to help in the war in any way. They talked a long time without getting anywhere about duty to the state and party leadership and highest expediency. In the end Mr. Cooper made him promise not to take any rash step without consulting him. [Note that Dick has now "decided" that his "principles" forbid him to enter any war work.] Back in Cambridge everybody was drilling and going to lectures on military science. Dick was finishing up the four year course in three years and had to work hard, but nothing in the courses seemed to mean anything any more. He managed to find time to polish up a group of sonnets called Morituri Te Salutant that he sent to a prize competition run by *The Literary Digest*. It won the prize but the editors wrote back that they would prefer a note of hope in the last sestet. Dick put in the note of hope [so go the words!] and sent the hundred dollars to Mother to go to Atlantic City with. He discovered that if he went into war work he could get his degree that spring without taking

any exams and went in to Boston one day without saying anything to anybody and signed up in the volunteer ambulance service. [Now he has "decided" that his "principles" no longer prevent him from war work.] (*1919*,
95–96)

And here is the sound of a Dos Passos character "deciding"
to have an abortion:

Of course she could have the baby if she wanted to [Don Stevens said] but
it would spoil her usefulness in the struggle for several months and he
didn't think this was the time for it. It was the first time they'd quarreled.
She said he was heartless. He said they had to sacrifice their personal feelings for the workingclass, and stormed out of the house in a temper. In
the end she had an abortion but she had to write her mother again for
money to pay for it. (*Big Money*, 447)

These examples of important decisions presented as simply
something that the character happened somehow to do are not
exceptional; they are typical. I think I can say safely that there
are *no* decisions in the three novels that are presented in a significantly different way.

To this extent, then, *U.S.A.* is systematically, rigidly, effectively deterministic. But there is a fault in its rigid structure, a
softness in its determinism, and—in opposition to both the friendly
and unfriendly critics of Dos Passos—I would suggest that a large
part of the book's success comes precisely from the author's failure
to be as consistently deterministic as he thinks he wants to be.
True as it is that we never identify with any of his characters
as we do with conventionally free characters, it is equally true
that we do not regard them all with the nice objectivity required
by the deterministic logic. Some we consider "good" and some
"bad," just as though they were in fact responsible human beings
making free choices. And these judgments that we make, however
illogically, we base largely upon the way in which the different
characters treat those crucial abstract words.

Some characters are essential neutral—or perhaps I should
say that we feel them to be truly determined. We look upon
Margo Dowling, Eveline Hutchins, Eleanor Stoddard, and Charley Anderson with a coolly detached eye, even though we may
feel that in their various ways the women are somewhat bitchy.
And although Daughter, and Joe and Janey Williams tend to
arouse our sympathies, we view them quite dispassionately. Cer-

tainly we do not consider any of these as responsible moral agents. And none of them shows any inclination to be concerned with the words.

In contrast to the neutral characters are Mac, Ben Compton, and Mary French. Dos Passos likes them and makes us like them because they affirm the values which he holds and wishes his readers to accept. Each of them uses the words, tries to uphold the true meaning of the "old words," and fights to rebuild the ruined words. Although their decisions are described in the same way that all other decisions are, we feel that their choices of the words are deliberate, and are acts of freedom for which they take the responsibility. Mac leaves his girl in San Francisco to go to Goldfield as a printer for the Wobblies because he finds that his life is meaningless when he is not using and acting out the words. Later, after his marriage, he escapes again from the bourgeois trap because he can't bear not to be talking with his old comrades about their dream and ideals. Finally, unable to do anything but talk and unable to find a way to make the old words new or effective, he sinks back into the conventional rut of the other unfree characters. Ben Compton insists on talking peace and socialism after the United States has entered the war, freely choosing thereby to be taken by the police and imprisoned. During the war, it seems, the old words may not be used in public until they have been converted into the official lies.

Mary French is generally considered Dos Passos's most sympathetic character in *U.S.A.* She is certainly associated with the words throughout, and in her work with the 1919 steel strikers and the Sacco-Vanzetti committee she is actively engaged in the attempt to "renew" the words and make them effective in the fight for justice. But, significantly, she does not employ them much. Not only have they been worn slimy in the mouths of her enemies, but they are continually being perverted by her co-workers and supposed friends, the ostensible renovators of the words. So, in the final section of *The Big Money,* we find her collecting clothes for the struck coal miners, doing good, but not a good that goes beyond the mere maintenance of brute existence. Anything of more significance would demand use of the words, and at this point in his writing, the words, to Dos Passos, have been ruined beyond redemption.

And then there are the bad guys, J. Ward Moorehouse and Richard Ellsworth Savage. They are as hollow as any other Dos Passos men, their decisions, like all others, non-decisions. But where Joe and Janey Williams make us sad, these make us mad. We dislike them and blame them, just as though they had really chosen.

Dos Passos makes us feel that a character is responsible for the words he chooses. To explain just *how* Dos Passos does that is not easy, but I think it goes, in part, something like this. We don't blame Dick for drinking too much or for wenching, any more than we blame Charley Anderson or Joe Williams. These activities seem to be instinctive reactions, self-defeating but natural escapes from freedom. Part of the reason we feel Dick and the others determined in their dissipation, and consequently do not blame them, is because the characters blame themselves, regret what they do and feebly resolve not to do it again. Thus when they fall back into their old, familiar ways, we feel that they are doing what they do not want to do, do not will to do. But when we come to another sort of action, the choice of words, no character is shown regretting the abstract words he uses. Thus the character implicitly approves his choice of words, he seems to be acting freely, and we tend to hold him responsible.

To get back to our bad guys, Moorehouse and Savage are the successful exploiters in the trilogy, and on first thought we might assume that that fact would suffice to make them culpable. But they are not the usual exploiters found in proletarian novels: big bad businessmen gouging the workers, manufacturers grinding the faces of the poor. Indeed they don't seem to hurt anyone. They exploit not people but words, or people, impersonally, by means of the words. Their profession is "public relations." (We might look at them as precursors of the Madison Avenue villains of post-World War II fiction, and infinitely superior ones, at that.) Their job is to persuade people to buy a product or to act in a particular way. Their means of persuasion is words. And the words they use are to a great extent "the words," the words of the American dream. They talk cooperation, justice, opportunity, freedom, equality.

Here are two brief quotations from J. Ward Moorehouse. He and Savage are preparing a publicity campaign for old Doc Bingham's patent medicines—now called "proprietary" medicines. (You will remember that Doc was Mac's first employer at the beginning of the trilogy, as owner-manager of "The Truthseeker Literary Distributing Co., Inc.") The first quotation is part of J. W.'s argument to a complaisant senator: "But, senator, . . . it's the principle of the thing. Once government interference in business is established as a precedent it means the end of liberty and private initiative in this country. . . . What this bill purports to do is to take the right of selfmedication from the American people" (505–506). And in this next one he is talking to his partner Savage about the advertising—no, publicity—campaign: "Of course self-service, independence, individualism is the word I gave the boys in the beginning. This is going to be more than a publicity campaign, it's going to be a campaign for Americanism" (494).

Here at last we have arrived at the source—or at least one major source—of the cancerous evil that swells malignantly through the books. Here we observe the manufacturers of the all-pervasive lies busily at work, here we see the words being deliberately perverted. And we cannot consider the perverters of the words as merely helpless automatons or innocents; they deliberately choose their words and we judge them as villains.

So, in conclusion, Dos Passos finds that the old words of the immigrant haters of oppression, which should have set Americans free, have instead been worn slimy in their mouths. And these words are in effect central actors in *U.S.A.* They determine our attitudes toward the characters who use and misuse them, establish the tone of hollow futility that rings throughout the trilogy, and leave in our mouths the bitter after-taste of nausea. The novels that followed, to make the *District of Columbia* trilogy, emphasize Dos Passos's sick obsession with these words. In the first, the humanitarian socialist dream comes to us in the clichés and jargon of American communists; in the second, the American dream is conveyed to us through the demagogery of a vulgar Louisiana dictator; in the third the dream of New Deal reform has been turned into a nightmare by cynical opportunists and time-serving bureaucrats who exploit the old words anew.

No longer able to imagine a way of giving to words their original meanings, after *U.S.A.,* Dos Passos could still not abandon them for some more palatable subject. And so he seemed to take the worst part of the worlds of Yevtushenko and Hemingway. But in *U.S.A.* he could still write about Mac and Ben Compton and Mary French; he could still feel some hope that the ruined words might be rebuilt; he could still imagine the dream to be yet a possibility. In *U.S.A.* his despair was not yet total and his dual vision of the words brought to these novels a tension, a vitality, and a creative energy he would never be able to muster again.

◆SHERWOOD CUMMINGS

What Is Man?: The Scientific Sources

MARK TWAIN's *What Is Man?* has been regarded as a kind of curiosity, and one can see why. In the first place its elaborately demonstrated doctrine that man is a will-less machine born with set capabilities and thereafter shaped by external influences seems to have little relevance to the explicit ideas or implicit themes in the main body of Mark Twain's work. In the second place, the humanist scholar finds the idea of determinism insignificant and repugnant. It cannot be taken seriously. If man is indeed a mechanism, then the study of mankind must be turned altogether over to the scientists.

Most of the comments on *What Is Man?*, therefore, have been casual and impressionistic. They deal in subjective and personal reasons for Mark Twain's writing his "gospel." The main such reasons are that Mark Twain's determinism is a remnant of his boyhood religion, a God-less predestination or an "inverted Calvinism";[1] that he denied man's responsibility for his actions so as to relieve his own sense of guilt;[2] and that it was written "as an attack upon human pride" and "the smug self-righteousness of bourgeois Protestant society."[3]

Of these reasons, that of Mark Twain's intention to puncture pride is consonant with the tenor of his other work and has been well supported by Alexander Jones's analysis. The other two are difficulty of final demonstration and the first one, that of "inverted Calvinism," seems to me wholly without supporting evidence. Although young Sam Clemens responded to such Calvinistic concepts as the sinfulness of man and his liability to damnation, the idea of predestination simply made no impression on him. Neither in the way that Tom Sawyer or Huck Finn thought about religion nor in Clemens's recollections of his own religious attitude is there the notion that men's careers had been divinely foreordained. The disposition of the soul was felt to be neither comfortably nor desperately predetermined; instead it was a matter of constant concern to its owner and to a large extent his responsibility.

Valid subjective reasons for Mark Twain's writing *What Is Man?* are interesting, but by themselves are misleading. They suggest that *What Is Man?* is an eccentric work which can be explained on the basis of Mark Twain's peculiar complex of experiences, that it stands apart not only from his major writing but from any considerable literary or philosophical preoccupation. I know of no study, for example, that attempts to correlate Mark Twain's deterministic ideas with those of Stephen Crane, Theodore Dreiser, or Ambrose Bierce. From a good deal of the pertinent scholarship one might conclude that these authors were conscious participants in a broad literary movement based on the scientific ideas of their time and that Mark Twain somehow stumbled into the same area because he had a Calvinistic upbringing and a guilt complex.

Professors H. H. Waggoner and Alexander Jones have, it is true, stated that the deterministic ideas of *What Is Man?* find support in current scientific speculation,[4] but little attempt has been made to find out whose ideas Mark Twain used and how he used them. The search for sources yields surprising results. The hundred-plus science-related books and articles that Mark Twain read provide a plethora of the ideas he needed to write *What Is Man?* and five in particular appear to be his immediate sources.

What one discovers is that the formation of Mark Twain's deterministic ideas, far from being peculiar, was in the classical pattern. The pattern is this: First one accepts the central revelation of Newtonian science, that the universe obeys perfectly orderly and infrangible laws. The universe is an exquisitely precise mechanism. The idea is at first exhilarating, for it frees one from the fear of capricious divine intervention and from various other superstitions. Then one observes that the scientists of his own century are quite logically tracing the iron authority of universal law through the most intimate workings of nature, and it becomes clear that if one accepts the principle of an orderly and ineluctable chain of causality in the whole he must admit its operation in all its parts, including human thought and behavior. Man is, after all, a creature of nature, another mechanism in the universal machine.

The influences that led to the final composition of *What Is Man?* operated on Mark Twain during the whole of his adult career. They began with his reading Thomas Paine's *Age of Reason* when he was a cub pilot. That book is monumentally important in his thinking, and precise echoes from it appear throughout his writing. In the early eighties, for example, he wrote as part of his credo, "I believe that the universe is governed by strict and immutable laws."[5]

With such preparation it is not surprising that when he read *The Autocrat of the Breakfast Table* in 1869[6], he should respond vividly to Oliver Wendell Holmes's assertion that "the more we study the body and the mind, the more we find both to be governed not *by* but *according to* laws, such as we observe in the larger universe."[*] In *The Autocrat*, which he read very carefully and whose margins he marked, he would come across Holmes's description of the mind as "intellectual mechanism" (130), "good mental machinery . . . with its own wheels and levers" (142), and "mental clockwork" (190–191). In *What Is Man?* Mark Twain repeated Holmes's idea by saying, "I think the mind is purely a machine, a thoroughly independent machine, an automatic machine."[†] The mind, Mark Twain continued, "is independent of the man. He has no control over it; it does as it pleases" (65). Again he echoed Holmes who wrote that "our will cannot stop 'the wheels of thought'; they cannot stop themselves; sleep cannot still them. . . . If we could only get at them, as we lie on our pillows and count the dead beats of thought after thought and image after image jarring through the overtired organ. . . . If anybody would only contrive some kind of lever that one could thrust in among

---

[*]*The Autocrat of the Breakfast Table* (Boston, 1891), p. 71. Hereafter quotations from this book are documented parenthetically in the text.

[†]*What is Man? and Other Essays* (New York, 1917), p. 68. Hereafter page references to this book are given parenthetically in the text.

the works of this horrid automaton and check them, . . . what would the world give for its discovery?" (185–187). Mark Twain's description of the Old Man's insomnia is strikingly similar: The mind "is diligently at work, unceasingly at work, during every waking moment. Have you never tossed about all night, imploring, beseeching, commanding your mind to stop work and let you go to sleep?—you who perhaps imagine that your mind is your servant and must obey orders . . ." (63).

Other parallels between *The Autocrat* and *What Is Man?* can be cited to monotony, but their gist can be summarized: Both the anatomist and the humorist called the creative process "automatic and involuntary";[7] Mark Twain denied free will and Holmes called it almost non-existent (86); both identified heredity and environment as the shapers of personality;[8] and both rather paradoxically admonished the reader to build more stately mansions, or, as Mark Twain expressed it, to "train your ideals *upward* . . ." (54–55).

The correspondence between Holmes's determinism and Mark Twain's is striking, but not all of the ideas in *What Is Man?* appear in *The Autocrat*. For the remainder Mark Twain depended on further reading.

Three years after he read *The Autocrat*, that is, in the winter of 1871–1872, Mark Twain read Darwin's *The Descent of Man*. The scholarly zeal with which he tackled Darwin's exposition of the origin of man and of man's kinship to the animals is evident in Clemens's marginalia in his copy of the book in the Mark Twain Papers. *The Descent of Man* afforded Mark Twain two major ideas later to appear in *What Is Man?* One of them concerns man's moral nature; the other the close relationship of man and the animals.

In *What Is Man?* Mark Twain declared that man's impulses are invariably selfish and that he is motivated by self-satisfaction and public opinion. Every act of apparent self-sacrifice can be explained as gratification of an inner need. The mother's starving and going naked to give her child food and clothing is done for "self approval, . . . contentment, . . . peace, . . . [and] comfort" (19). Darwin had made a similar analysis: The sight of suffering, he said, arouses sympathetic feelings in the onlooker. "We are thus impelled to relieve the sufferings of another, in order that

our own painful feelings may be at the same time relieved."* Next
to this passage in his copy of *The Descent of Man* Mark Twain
wrote to the effect that what seems like generosity is only selfishness.

Both writers noted man's need to accommodate himself to
public pressures. Wrote Darwin: Man is "influenced in the highest
degree by the wishes, approbation, and blame of his fellow men
. . ." (109). "Even when an action is opposed to no special instinct, merely to know that our friends and equals despise us for it
is enough to cause great misery. Who can doubt that the refusal
to fight a duel through fear has caused many a man an agony of
shame?" (114) Much of what Mark Twain said is in the same
vein; for example: "Public opinion can force some men to do
anything. . . . Alexander Hamilton was a conspicuously high-
principled man. He regarded dueling as wrong, and as opposed
to the teaching of religion—but in deference to public opinion he
fought a duel" (16–17).

Fourteeen of the 109 pages of *What Is Man?* are devoted to
the equating of man's intellectual machinery with that of animals.
Mark Twain's conclusion in these pages, that "there is absolutely
no intellectual frontier separating Man and the Unrevealed Creatures" (88), is similar to Darwin's in Chapter 3, which begins,
"My object in this chapter is to shew that there is no fundamental
difference between man and the higher mammals in their mental
faculties" (66), and Mark Twain borrowed from Darwin several
bits of supporting evidence. Darwin, like Mark Twain, said that
animals reason and have a form of speech, and like Twain he saw
that the main difference between animals and man was man's
moral sense. Wrote Darwin: "The moral sense perhaps affords
the best and highest distinction between man and the lower animals" (126). The Young Man in *What Is Man?* echoes him in
declaring that "there is still a wall, and a lofty one. [Animals]
haven't got the Moral Sense; we have it, and it lifts us immeasurably above them" (89). The Old Man agrees to the difference, but
shames mankind for neglecting to do what is right.

The admonition of *What Is Man?*, already referred to, that
you must "diligently train your ideals *upward* and *still upward*

The Descent of Man in Relation to Sex (New York, 1887), p. 106.
Subsequent page references in parentheses are to this edition.

toward a summit where you will find your chiefest pleasure in conduct which, while contenting you, will be sure to confer benefits upon your neighbor and the community" (54) seems again to be an echo from Darwin, who wrote: "Man prompted by his conscience, will through long habit acquire such perfect self-command, that his desires and passions will at last yield instantly and without struggle to his social sympathies and instincts, including his feeling for the judgment of his fellows" (115).

Again only samples of the numerous parallels between the statements in *What Is Man?* and what must be called one of its major sources have been given. *The Autocrat* and *The Descent of Man,* indeed, express or imply every single idea that is contained in Mark Twain's "gospel." Nevertheless, two other books were influential and one other possibly so.

The first of these is W. E. H. Lecky's *History of European Morals from Augustus to Charlemagne,* which Mark Twain read in 1874. The book is important for the likelihood that it suggested the dialogue structure of *What is Man?*. Lecky's first chapter, comprising one sixth of the book, defines and produces arguments for and against two schools of moral philosophy: the utilitarian school which holds that man's motives are selfish and that morals are the product of social experience, and the intuitive school (to which Lecky belonged) which maintains that conscience is a divine gift. The debate between these two schools is precisely the one that the Young Man and the Old Man engage in during several pages of *What Is Man?*. It is the Young Man who is the intuitivist and the Old Man who is the utilitarian. The Young Man's arguments and questions—for example, "Do you believe in the doctrine that man is equipped with an intuitive perception of good and evil?" (47)—follow very closely Lecky's own views and are overwhelmed by the Old Man's utilitarian and deterministic logic, closely paralleled in Lecky's explications of the opposition's arguments.

To be mentioned briefly is John Lubbock's *Ants, Bees, and Wasps,* of which Mark Twain owned two copies and which he read in 1882 and again in 1896. Mark Twain used data from Lubbock's book to prove that evidences of formic intelligence abolish "the intellectual frontier between man and beast" (82). That conclusion is more extreme than Lubbock's, which is that ants "have a fair claim to rank next to man in the scale of intelligence,"[9] and to close the gap between the two conclusions Mark Twain sometimes dramatically manipulated the evidence.

Finally to be mentioned is Thomas Huxley's essay *Evolution and Ethics*.* It again expresses all the major ideas in *What Is Man?*—that "man, physical, intellectual, and moral, is as much a part of nature, as purely a product of the cosmic process, as the humblest weed" and that all living things are "working out their predestined courses of evolution" (7), that the mind can be obsessed "by ideas which cannot be obliterated by any effort of the will" (11), that men are closely related to the other animals (26), that men are motivated by "their innate desire to enjoy the pleasures and to escape the pains of life" (27), that men are constrained by public disapproval (29), that personality is formed by heredity and environment (44, 61–62), and that man must train his ideals upward because a virtuous life is an advantage both to the individual and society (81–83). Huxley's *Evolution and Ethics* was published in 1894, four years before Mark Twain did most of the writing of *What Is Man?*. We know that Mark Twain read the essay but we do not know when.[10] *Evolution and Ethics* may not have been an influence on *What Is Man?* but a corroboration of Mark Twain's ideas.

Obviously Mark Twain swam during his whole career in the mainstream of ideas that produced the naturalistic writers. The question of the relationship of *What Is Man?* to the main body of his work now becomes more urgent. At first glance there will seem to be little connection between the doctrine of determinism expressed in *What Is Man?* and the import of Mark Twain's novels. Only *The Mysterious Stranger*, written in the *What Is Man?* period, can be called a fictional restatement of the notion that men's lives are shaped by inexorable internal and external forces in which the human will plays no part. One answer to the question of why Mark Twain did not write explicitly deterministic novels during a whole career when he was absorbing deterministic ideas is that those ideas in their gradual accumulation did not dominate his thinking until late in life. Another answer is that Mark Twain, a man of many minds, could reason in one way and write in another.

*The parenthetical page references documenting the text are to *Evolution and Ethics and Other Essays* (New York, 1903).

He was a second-rate thinker, but at his best a great creative artist. Although *What Is Man?* is simplistic and doctrinaire as an intellectual statement, his considerable novels (unlike those of some naturalists) transcend doctrine. As an artist he was, as Howells said, "unconscious,"[11] meaning that he was in command of resources much deeper than the rational. As an artist and as a man of action he did not believe in absolute determinism any more than the Puritan who carried a gun to church because he might meet an Indian whose time had come. Although early in life he acquiesced intellectually in the deterministic ideas implicit in current science, he knew intuitively that a novel written to demonstrate the doctrine that man is a will-less machine would be as meaningless as the doctrine itself. When late in life there was a closer accommodation between his reason and his creative impulses, his imagination became or had become crippled.

Nevertheless there is no hermetic division between what Mark Twain thought and what his imagination created in the long noon of his career. Several of his novels may, indeed, be regarded as explorations in the human meaning of one of the tenets of his "gospel"—that environment molds character. "It is his human environment," he wrote in *What Is Man?*, "which influences [a man's] mind and his feelings, furnishes him his ideals. . . . The influences about him create his preferences, his aversions, his politics, his tastes, his morals, his religion" (43). Professor Gladys Bellamy has shown that as early as the writing of *The Prince and the Pauper* (1881), in which the author paid "attention to the pressure of environment upon the moral fiber of the small bogus prince, Tom Canty of Offal Court," Mark Twain was giving fictional form to a facet of his deterministic theory, and that he continued to do so in *A Connecticut Yankee* and *Pudd'nhead Wilson*.[12] *Adventures of Huckleberry Finn* is equally concerned with the problem of environment and character: the irony of the novel arises from the conflict within Huck between his good heart and his village-trained conscience and in the larger view between the comparatively uncivilized and therefore innocent Huck and those people along the River who have become demeaned and corrupted by the prevailing culture. In *What Is Man?* Mark Twain stated the doctrine of determinism that he had constructed from his science reading; from his novels a part of that doctrine may be inferred, but it has been appropriately translated into fictional terms. Perhaps Mark Twain sensed the equation that doctrine over art equals dreariness.

NOTES

[1]Edward Wagenknecht, *Mark Twain: The Man and His Work* (New Haven, 1935), p. 216.

[2]*Ibid.,* pp. 244–245; Carl Van Doren, *The American Novel, 1789–1939* (New York, 1940), p. 157.

[3]Alexander E. Jones, "Mark Twain and the Determinism of *What Is Man?*", *American Literature,* XXIX (1957), 11.

[4]*Ibid.,* pp. 4–7; H. H. Waggoner, "Science in the Thought of Mark Twain," *American Literature,* VIII (1937), 360–361.

[5]Albert Bigelow Paine, *Mark Twain, A Biography* (New York, 1912), p. 1583.

[6]Bradford A. Booth, "Mark Twain's Comments on Holmes's *Autocrat,*" *American Literature,* XXI (1950), 456.

[7]Holmes, p. 191; Clemens, p. 8. The quoted phrase is Twain's. Holmes wrote: "The creative action is not voluntary at all, but automatic."

[8]Holmes, p. 98; Clemens, pp. 4, 48, *et passim.*

[9]*Ants, Bees, and Wasps* (New York, 1901), p. 1.

[10]Waggoner, p. 362.

[11]*Mark Twain–Howells Letters,* ed. Henry Nash Smith and William M. Gibson (Cambridge, Mass., 1960), p. 241.

[12]*Mark Twain as a Literary Artist* (Norman, 1950), pp. 310–323.